# BRADMAN

*What
They
Said
About
Him*

*Queen Anne Press*

BARRY MORRIS

# CONTENTS

The author and publisher wish to thank the Bradman Museum for permission to reproduce its exhibits in various ways throughout this book. We are grateful, in particular, for the opportunity to arrange the special image which is the frontispiece of this book.

A QUEEN ANNE PRESS BOOK

First published in 1994 by
Queen Anne Press, a division of
Lennard Associates Ltd
Mackerye End, Harpenden
Herts AL5 5DR

British Library Cataloguing in Publication Data
is available

ISBN 1 85291 5641

*For my family*

# FOREWORD

It is an honour for me to write the foreword to this book: *Bradman: What They Said About Him*. I am not a former cricketer of note, nor did I ever see Sir Donald play. I am one of the growing body of admirers who were born after he retired from first-class cricket.

Although it is now over 45 years since Sir Donald last graced the cricket field, you would be excused for thinking it was only yesterday. Such was the magnitude of his achievements as a player, that his name stands head and shoulders above anyone else who has ever played the game. For 20 years Sir Donald dominated the game, capturing the imagination of the cricketing world. As a batsman he was supreme, retiring with a Test average of 99.94. But it was more than his extraordinary batting which made him stand out. It was his remarkable demeanour on and off the field. He led Australia with grace, dedication and distinction.

He has given his life to the game and in doing so has set an example for all to follow. Sir Donald has impressed upon us the possibility of re-writing the record books in whatever field of endeavour we choose. It is this example which helped establish the Bradman Museum, which is dedicated to honouring Sir Donald and those who have played with him. It will preserve their memory, as well as actively promoting the principles that cricket stands for.

To quote Alan Jones from this book 'To have missed a Bradman innings is a quirk of fate; to have known the man is an extension of privelege'. Like Alan, it has been my good fortune to claim Sir Donald as a friend. He has given his full support to the Museum, recognising that it is to be a tribute to all that have played the game. Throughout his life he has maintained a great sense of humility and fair play. He has been largely unaffected by the publicity he has generated. Without doubt he is our greatest living Australian.

This book, which is a unique collection of quotes about Sir Donald, will, like the Museum, be a lasting testimony to his great contribution. Barry Morris has compiled over 1000 quotes, which together tell the Bradman story as never told before. It includes comments from many great cricketers who have known him well, through to newspaper journalists who would have liked to.

I congratulate ABC Books for producing a book which will be a great addition to any cricket library. After you have read it, you too will have a new insight into the man, not just the cricketer, of whom Sir Robert Menzies said: 'As a pavilion lover of the greatest of all games, I have balanced up the Bradman account and hereby acknowledge that, so long as my memory lasts, I shall owe him that which I can never repay'.

Richard Mulvaney
*Director Bradman Museum*

"Small Autograph-Hunter.
"HAVE YOU GOT BRADMAN?"
Smaller Autograph-Hunter.
"NO, BUT I'VE GOT THE SIGNATURE
OF A CHAP THAT HAS."

## THE HERO
### Sport's First Superstar

'Don Bradman's singular achievement
is that he became sport's first superstar
in an age when word-of-mouth was the
alternative to today's action replay.'

MICHAEL PARKINSON

*1*

## L AMARNARTH

Never was a more befitting tribute paid to a great cricketing personality.

*(on Bradman's knighthood)*

I love to play against him, and that goes for all my players, because he is such a great sportsman and a thorough gentleman.

## JOHN ARLOTT

Crowds flocked to see, not basically the Australian touring team, despite its powers, but Bradman.

There are certain players whom ordinary people, often not very interested in cricket in general, will pay to see. Undoubtedly the greatest such attraction in recent years was the Australian Sir Donald Bradman.

Bradman has planted himself in the minds of men who follow cricket.

W G Grace was a great Victorian figure in England; but at a pinch he was simply a cricketer. He was admired, but never knew the adulation that 'the Don' has aroused in his own country.

## 'AURELIUS'

*... today he is the acclaimed champion batsman of the world, holder of almost every record in the game, the idol of one nation, and the source of wonderment to others.*

The world is at the feet of Don Bradman. The English-speaking and cricket-loving nations are worshipping at the shrine of this unassuming boy from Bowral.

### AUSTRALIAN SPOUSE

If you don't stop that durn radio I'll sue for divorce and name your hero, Don Bradman, as primary cause of cruelty and neglect.

### E H M BAILLIE

No player, not even the immortal Victor Trumper, has captured the imagination of the public as has Bradman . . .

### LORD BALDWIN

Bradman the cricketer is known to all the English-speaking world, but Bradman the man I hope I may call my friend.

### S G BARNES

*All they wanted to write about was 'the Don'. No need for him to chase publicity. It chased him.*

I worshipped him. He could do nothing wrong as far as I was concerned . . .

. . . in conferring upon Don Bradman the dignity of a knighthood, authority has placed a laurel wreath upon the brow of its most distinguished son in sport.

### PERCY BEAMES

Nothing could have been more fitting than that the world's greatest batsman should say farewell to cricket with such an unforgettable 123 as Bradman made on Saturday.

## A BEDSER

I thought the reception he received at Headingley would be impossible to beat, but the Oval crowd did Don prouder still.

## A J BELL

He is one of the most magnetic personalities I have ever met in the course of my cricket career.

## R BENAUD

Bradman as a young man had the magic to bring crowds pouring back to the game—probably more so than any other cricketer in the history of the game.

He was the batsman, in fact the cricketer in the world, and everyone wanted to know him, write about him and be associated with him in some way.

## SIR WILLIAM NORMAN BIRKETT

The great warrior was putting off his harness, and the crowds were anxious to show him their abiding gratitude for the pleasure he had given to countless thousands, to render homage to his greatness, and to express their admiration and affection for the way he had borne himself amidst the world's acclamation.

Never, never have I heard more tragic words fall from the lips of any man.

*(on Bradman's retirement)*

## MRS E BRADMAN *(mother)*

*If Don breaks any more records I don't know how I will manage to get through the clerical work involved in answering congratulations.*

4

### GEORGE BRADMAN *(father)*

*Are we proud of him? Well, don't you think we ought to be?*

### LADY BRADMAN

He has never looked on himself as a celebrity, and so his knighthood never made any difference to us.

### BRADMAN SCRAPBOOKS

Such hero worship comes to few men in their time.

### AUSTEN BROWN

*Don has thrilled us on a hundred cricket fields and has made us proud that we are Australians.*

. . . no one has ever equalled him in filling the public stands.

No man has captured the imagination of the cricket lover more completely or given us greater pleasure than Don . . .

### W A BROWN

The effect that Don had on the crowd was amazing ... It is hard to describe to people who weren't born in that era.

The knighthood is a wonderful tribute to a man who has given everything to the game.

### LINDSAY BROWNE

For it was clear from the earliest days that Bradman, out of shyness and out of honesty, wasn't much given to the pleasant little hypocrisies and glad-handling by which 'popularity' can be so easily bought.

## ALEX BUZO

In the end he became a myth himself and took his place somewhere between the earth-bound dog on the tucker box and Sir Charles Kingsford Smith. He will be in the pantheon for a good while yet.

He shouldered arms to the fuss being made over him in Fleet Street and as a teetotaller he felt no need to cash in on his fame in the flesh pots of Leeds.

Along with Charles Chaplin, he is one of the Untarnished Angels.

## A A CALDWELL

I will do my best to see that the fame of Don Bradman is at least enhanced in the eyes of the Australian people . . .

## 'CAPE TIMES' *(headline)*

```
        B
        R
        A
B R A D M A N
        M
        A
        N
```

## SIR NEVILLE CARDUS

*At Adelaide, there was, we suspected, likely to be a beautiful wicket and hot weather; 100 in the shade and Bradman 300 in the sun.*

Bradman's achievements stagger the imagination. No writer of boy's fiction would dare to invent a 'hero' who performed with Bradman's continual consistency.

. . . crowds came from far and near to see him, and departed in disappointed droves when he got out.

Bradman was heralded with trumpets and trombones of acclamation as he walked to the wicket, and the whole of the multitude's orchestra crashed out as he cut Allen for four and pulled him gigantically for four.

A large crowd assembled on the pretty Worcester ground to see Bradman and others. There were some 11 000 of them, and everybody breathed on everybody else's neck, and pushed and trod and elbowed.

### CLIF CARY

*No one in the history of the game has made turnstiles click so frantically as Bradman.*

### RICHARD CASHMAN

I compared the daily crowds when Bradman was involved in 74 days of Shield cricket . . . the average attendance on the 41 days when he batted was 14 557, whereas the average when he did not bat was only 7 627.

### SIR WINSTON CHURCHILL

Isn't that Bradman you are with? I'd like to be introduced.

*(to Tom Clarke)*

### ROY COLMER

A crowd of 52 960 greeted Don Bradman with one of the greatest receptions ever given an Australian sportsman when he walked out to bat in his testimonial game at Melbourne Cricket Ground today.

## D C S COMPTON

I 'got' Bradman, and in years to come will be able to tell my son, Brian, that his father once sent back to the pavilion the wonderful Don Bradman.

## CLAUDE CORBETT

It was Don Bradman's day, and he came in all his glory to wind himself around the hearts of the cricket public with his dashing batsmanship.

After the game old men who sat in the stands went away muttering to themselves at the miracle of batsmanship they had witnessed.

## GERRY COTTER

He is revered above everyone in Australia, and rightly so, for his achievements did, after all, transcend those of everyone else who ever picked up a cricket bat.

## M C COWDREY

As he walked back to the pavilion for the last time, having made 150, he turned to the crowd, hung his gloves around his bat handle, raised them aloft and bowed farewell. I don't think that I have ever seen a more moving moment than this on the cricket field . . .

To have met and come to know Don Bradman is one of the real privileges arising from my cricket travels to Australia.

## FRANK CUSH

To me, Don is more than a member of the Australian XI, having lived in my house for the last 12 to 18 months, and I describe him as one of the finest characters that ever graced a cricket field.

### 'DAILY EXPRESS'

*The crowd came to see Don Bradman bat, and for preference, to knock up 100 or so. Will bowlers please note that getting Bradman out for a duck should be reserved for Test matches only.*

Hail to Sir Don Bradman, best batsman in the world and most able cricket captain.

### 'DAILY HERALD'

As soon as the day's play had ended, the crowds converge on the hotel, most of them armed with autograph books and pen, and generally it is Bradman they want.

### 'DAILY MAIL'

The public in this country can appreciate a brilliant antagonist, and in the ranks of famous Australian cricketers there has been none more brilliant than Bradman.

Sir Don Bradman. The great man of cricket today receives a knighthood from the King . . . The honour comes at the close of 40-year-old Bradman's career as the most brilliant batsman and captain of his generation.

When he came in there was a rush, especially of women, to pat him on the back. Although women are great cricket fans in Australia, I have never seen so many at a cricket match in England.

### 'DAILY MIRROR'

Hail, Sir Don. His knighthood brings the climax of an outstanding career that has captured and exhilarated boys of all ages.

. . . a local girl was nearly run over when she rushed across the road to throw a bat made from flowers through the window of Don Bradman's car.

### 'DAILY NEWS'

There is already a word 'Bradmanitis'. They even gag about him in the music halls; indeed, no music hall artist tops the bill like Bradman.

### 'DAILY PICTORIAL'

*Some teams are so anxious to see Bradman that they willingly send in Australia to bat just to watch him. This is unparalleled.*

That's Don Bradman, nonchalant, delightful, quiet, undemonstrative run-getter.

The King's illness would not cause much more excitement at the moment than the suggestion that Don Bradman is indisposed.

### 'DAILY TELEGRAPH'

Bradman has won every heart immediately by his confidence and the suggestion of immense physical strength, by his boyish face and fair hair.

Bradman is the particular idol of the crowd. No sooner do they settle in their seat than they ask 'Which is Don Bradman? Where is he fielding?'

### KEN DALBY

. . . with tens of thousands locked out and a record-breaking 39 000 within, waiting for witch-doctors Bradman and Yardley to dispense the magic willow-herb.

Headingley rose to his genius. They had not seen his like before.

Hail, Caesar! Bradman emerged with Ponsford to a tumultuous welcome and promptly despatched the last two balls of Bowe's incompleted over to the boundary . . .

### ANTHONY DAVIS

*County Club secretaries developed ulcers worrying about Bradman's health. If he played in a county game it could mean the end of the club's overdraft; if he had to withdraw it could mean higher red figures.*

The crowd, recognising Don, gave him an ovation that rivalled that for members of the Royal Family.

### J C DAVIS

That as many as 100 journalists, and half as many photographers, assembled at the Worcester ground indicates that no tour of the past ever had such intense public glare focused upon it.

The whole world applauded him. Australia listened in to a story, magnetic, entrancing, unparalleled.

### H A DE LACY

It was Bradman this, Bradman that. Always and forever we return to Bradman.

### PHILIP DERRIMAN

*He was the greatest crowd puller Australian sport has known.*

To a quite extraordinary degree Bradman's fame has survived the years and there is not one newspaper editor, for instance, who would not more eagerly grab the chance of an interview today with Sir Donald than with any modern champion.

### E W DOCKER

In Perth a huge mob took scarcely any notice of its other famous visitors, Richardson and McCabe, Fingleton and Lonergon. It had come to feast its eyes on Bradman alone. Police armed a way through the melee so that he could reach his hotel.

Despite the emergence of Lindwall and Miller, Barnes and Morris and so on, the world still craved the sight of Bradman, it seemed.

Everywhere people wanted to shake his hand, talk to him, become associated with him in some form or other, however fleeting.

To them he was only, affectionately, 'Braddles' and 'Braddles' he will always remain in their memories, though of course they cannot forget the crowds, the excitement, the lustre that his presence added to the game in those golden years.

### SIDNEY DOWNER

Latter-day spectators cannot know the electrifying and magnetic effect which Don Bradman exercised over the crowds of his playing period. They went to see Don Bradman. And they couldn't have cared less about anyone else. It was tough on the other players, but they just were not Bradman.

### KEITH DUNSTAN

*Then as soon as he was out, although it was before lunch, half the crowd left. No Bradman, no cricket, as far as they were concerned.*

As soon as the word went about that Bradman was making runs, crowds began to pour through the turnstiles.

### ENGLISH FAN

Oh! I don't want to watch Bradman! He's sure to make runs and be there all day. Let's have a glass of beer . . .

### 'ESSEX CHRONICLE'

It's not all fun being a cricket celebrity. Don Bradman is harassed by clamouring fans wherever he goes.

On Saturday he appeared almost unrecognised. By Monday he had to be brought to the ground by car, with two policeman hanging on each running-board to repel boarders.

### T G EVANS

The highlight of that Test was the last appearance of Don Bradman. As he walked out to the wicket, I shall never forget the thunder of cheering that went up.

### H V EVATT

I cannot part with the subject of this sketch without expressing gratitude for the infinite pleasure which Bradman's batting has given to all cricket lovers.

Despite all his honours, Donald Bradman is still as modest and unassuming as the young country lad who came to Sydney in 1927 intent upon success in the greatest of games.

## W H Ferguson

**Cricket can boast many princes but, in my experience, it has possessed only one king, Don Bradman.**

. . . having seen every Test match in which he played, I can say that not once did I hear him have any altercation with anyone.

## 'The Field'

All the obligation of fame surrounds Don Bradman at the present time. His daily post must be beyond the hopes of any film star . . .

## J H Fingleton

No prince could have had a more regal entry into Perth. As the long and dusty eastern train jolted to a stop, thousands crammed the station, the adjoining roofs and buildings, the exits and the streets outside.

When the train was on its long run across the Nullarbor Plain, lonely men and women of the outback travelled many miles to catch a glimpse of this cricket magician.

He was cheered to the echo whenever he appeared on the ground, and the people's faces lit up as if they had seen a miracle when they recognised him in the street.

At lonely outposts on the long, straight railway line, children clustered and called 'Bradman, Bradman' as the train rushed through the night.

People who had never been to a cricket match before, who did not know a bat from a ball, flocked to see Bradman.

Businessmen on the verge of bankruptcy said 'To hell with business', closed up their doors and went out to forget their woes and themselves with Bradman.

He was seen for the last time on an English field at Lord's in 1948 and thousands stood on the field for him to make an almost Royal appearance on the Australian balcony.

### ANDY FLANAGAN

To travel throughout England with Bradman is a unique experience. Cities, towns, and hotels are beflagged, carpets set down, and dignitaries wait to extend an official welcome. He is the Prince of Cricketers.

### MALCOLM FRASER

Mandela's first words to me were: 'Fraser, can you please tell me, is Donald Bradman still alive?'

### C B FRY

He has humour, too. A great asset. If only the Australian Board of Control would let him, he'd amuse us with words as well as shock us with runs.

### GEORGE V, KING

*It was a pleasure to His Majesty to meet him, to see them play, and to have the opportunity of watching Mr Bradman play.*

### A E R GILLIGAN

Don Bradman has always played cricket according to its highest traditions and he deserves the thanks of cricket lovers throughout the world.

Even his dressing-room was not sacred. People peered into windows, but Bradman was promptly shut off from view by sheets of brown paper.

Thousands were on their feet cheering him and waving hats on handkerchiefs. If he had been an Englishman, his reception could have been no greater.

### J D C GODDARD

The honour is an honour to cricket, but it is Sir Donald Bradman's achievements which have made it a deserving honour.

*(on Bradman's knighthood)*

### TOM GOODMAN

I have witnessed many memorable scenes in which Bradman has been the central figure. The reception accorded him yesterday was certainly one of the most vociferous and most sustained that has been given on this famous Sydney field.

### 'GUARDIAN'

Breaking the barriers, a wild crowd surged around the Australian Airways plane which brought Don Bradman from Adelaide.

Famous Don Bradman was cheered by perhaps a million people in the eight months he was away . . .

### I GUPTA

*We would prefer to lose every match and see Bradman play than win every match and not see him.*

## F J C GUSTARD

He will be the greatest 'draw' of the season.

## JOE HARDSTAFF

His last appearances up and down the country were more like the farewell performances of a beloved matinee idol.

## BRUCE HARRIS

*Three possessions lie nearest to the true Sydneyite's heart—'our 'arbour, our bridge, our Bradman'—and maybe I have placed the order wrong.*

In Australia the health of Bradman is as much a national concern as that of a racehorse like Bernborough . . .

I feel that if Bradman were reported to be dying he would still confound the news gatherers by turning out and scoring centuries.

At Koolgardie, west of the desert, a girl autograph hunter boarded the train with others and demanded 'Don'. She was shown his locked door. 'I'll stay here till he comes out', she declared. She did.

. . . the crowd at Perth station received him like a popular hero and almost forgot the others. Policemen had to ram a way for him through the mass.

## COLIN HAY

Of course, he did achieve such greatness that he became just plain Bradman. And such is fame that one can be known by surname alone!

## R J HAYTER

> *... and shortly before six o'clock Bradman walked to the wicket amidst continued applause from the standing crowd. Yardley shook hands with Bradman and called on the England team for three cheers, in which the crowd joined.*
>
> *(Bradman's last Test)*

The British public paid striking tribute to his popularity and they made such a big response to a newspaper fund for a Bradman testimonial that, after receiving a silver trophy, he asked that the surplus money should go towards the provision of pitches similar to those on which he learned his cricket.

## G A HEADLEY

It is a fitting tribute to a wonderful sportsman.

*(on Bradman's knighthood)*

## GEORGE HELE

Don was never one to gloat. I always found him most modest. What human being would not have been delighted to have been able to bat as he could?

## E H HENDREN

But I have put in the facts so that you may know the Bradman of today a trifle better; the hero who can and will do a favour for an unknown enthusiast.

## GERALD HOWAT

Bradman was by now an acclaimed hero and the crowds pursued him relentlessly after the match to the Oval tube station, onto the train, and to the entrance to his hotel at St Pancras.

No other person in any field of activity remotely approached Bradman in the public estimation. If one accepts the thesis that Australia—in the Depression years still a nation unsure of its identity—needed a folk hero, it was he.

### MARGARET HUGHES

Millions, who had not a notion of an off break or a square cut, knew him only as the International Bogeyman of cricket.

### W M HUGHES

Little more than a boy, his name was on all men's mouths. The crowd had come there to see him bat. They were not to be disappointed.

### SIR LEN HUTTON

The Bradman effect on me that unforgettable occasion at Headingley was magical.

### JACK INGHAM

*It is strange, but I think true, that all the time, day and night, somewhere in the world somebody is talking about Bradman.*

Everybody talks about Bradman. People who don't know one thing from the next in cricket all talk about him.

Round this time on Saturday, you will be talking, or thinking, of the little broad-shouldered, slow-speaking Australian.

### ALAN JONES

To have missed a Bradman innings is a quirk of fate; to have known the man is an extension of privilege . . .

In my inability to live through a Bradman innings, I have genuinely felt the Gods were against me.

### J M KILBURN

There was a silence of suspense; a murmur of 'He's here', swelling to a roar of welcome to greet the greatest cricketing figure of his time.

### HARRY KNEEBONE

*What was needed on top of warm sunshine and a record crowd for a match other than a Test, to make the day supremely successful, was a Bradman century. So he produced one.*

### A P E KNOTT

. . . I had the thrill of meeting Sir Donald and his wife for the first time . . . here was a vital personality, a man of 62 still bubbling with fitness and mental alertness.

### H LARWOOD

Don Bradman's reception was the greatest I have heard on any cricket field. The crowd cheered for five minutes. We just couldn't go on with the game.

Cricket fans of today have no idea how dynamic this little chap was.

### GWEN LEACH

*"Donbradmania'. H'm! Queer word.'*
*'Where did it originate?'*
*'Originate? Why, it is a disease.'*

## LAURENCE LE QUESNE

. . . and it would be hard to imagine a better image of the popular hero than the young, unpretentious Bradman, who could give vicarious form to the hopeful or frustrated ambitions of so many.

His autobiography—at the age of 21!—had already been published in instalments in an English evening paper during the tour.

Throngs awaited him wherever he went: he was given a car; a cinema was named after him; newspapers fought for the privilege of publishing his articles.

## LAWRIE LESLIE

Our own Don, the pride of Australia, a gentleman as Australians understood the meaning of the word.

## PHILIP LINDSAY

For I loved Don Bradman. At first I was ashamed of betrayal, clinging to Macartney, but soon I realised that I could love both men . . .

## R R LINDWALL

*Before I even set eyes on him I was a Bradman fan and, after watching him play for my local St George club, I became a still more fervent admirer.*

I never heard him say a word of criticism about anyone else in the game, player or official, and I never heard him complain about an umpire's decision.

## LONDON PAVEMENT ARTIST

Amy Johnson was a fair attraction, but Don—well, he seems to melt the 'earts o' nearly everyone these 'ard times!

## LONDON SOCIETY WOMAN

Oh! I've just been talking to Don Bradman. He is as shy as a gazelle and as modest as a buttercup. I felt like taking him in my arms and kissing him, he's so nice.

## H J LONG

I feel I must write to you to say I thank God I have been spared to witness the unforgettable scene at the Oval on Saturday when you emerged from the pavilion to take your place at the crease.

*(On Bradman's last Test appearance)*

## G F McCLEARY

It is not too much to say that the history of Anglo-Australian cricket in the period 1929–48 is largely a history of Don's achievements.

In the musical world 'the Don' is a colloquial name for Mozart's great opera, Don Giovanni. To lovers of cricket it is a name used to denote an illustrious and popular cricketer—Sir Donald Bradman.

## C L McCOOL

*I might as well come straight out and admit that I loved the bloke. As far as I am concerned he was fair, just and very human.*

### ALAN MCGILVRAY

As he came to the wicket for his last innings four policeman escorted him through lines of people four to six feet deep.

### A A MAILEY

Don Bradman is one of the biggest figures in the sporting world. He is a world figure, despite the fact that cricket and cricketers are almost unknown in certain countries.

. . . packed like sardines, hanging on to balcony, railing posts, trees, and every other vacant spot, forget their discomfort for a while, and looked forward to seeing the young champion stop the rot.

### JIM MATHERS

Every run he made was applauded. Every 10 he scored was noted. Every 50 was cheered. His century passed, and the crowd began to settle down for records.

The true story of the finding of Sir Donald George Bradman, capitalistic cricket colossus, who was knighted in the New Year's Honours list by a King, reads like a Nat Gould thriller.

### SIR ROBERT MENZIES

As a pavilion lover of the greatest of all games, I have balanced up the Bradman account and hereby acknowledge that, so long as my memory lasts, I shall owe him that which I can never repay.

### P J MILLARD

*Whenever the first wicket fell in Don's side, the air became electric, and the crowd buzzed with expectation. For the great Don Bradman was next to bat, in his traditional role of No 3.*

... no man going out to bat on the MCG has ever had such a reception.

### A R MORRIS

Don Bradman brought happiness to thousands of people.

### A G MOYES

Was Don Bradman to bat? If so, the ground was full. Press and public lauded him to the skies.

The plain fact is that Don Bradman without his records, his bat, and his pads, is an ordinary citizen just like the thousands who live in any of our suburbs and who are the basis of all decent society.

When my book *Bradman* was published some critics suggested hero-worship. Nonsense. Admiration? Yes. Doesn't he deserve that? I think so.

As a man he was—and is—kindly and lovable, generous where he gives his friendship but careful in bestowing it.

In January 1926, Don Bradman, aged 17, was employed in an estate agent's business in a little country town in New South Wales ... In January 1949, he was Sir Donald Bradman, successful sharebroker, director of companies, a world figure.

### PATRICK MURPHY

*From 1930—his first tour of England—till his retirement in 1949, Bradman was in the driving seat, and the rest nowhere.*

## M A NOBLE

What an eye this youth must have! What an inspiration to the youth of Australia! What an asset to our national game!

Don was the real magnet today. Bradman is the greatest batsman in the world, and the most popular drawcard, yet, with all his skill and popularity, he is one of the most modest and unassuming players who ever lived.

## A D NOURSE

Sir Donald Bradman brought a personality into the game which will be remembered as long as cricket, indeed sport, is cherished.

## 'OBSERVER'

Bradman was now the greatest figure in world sport.

## W A OLDFIELD

*... street urchins clambered onto the running-board of Bradman's car just to catch a glimpse of him, and to greet him with their shrill tribute.*

The colossal performances made him a public idol from Royalty down to the newsboys in the street.

At Lord's, during the Test match of 1930, the late King George was viewing the match from the Committee Room. So interested was he that when reminded of an important engagement in London he declared that he would not leave the ground until Bradman had completed his century.

## W J O'Reilly

His presence in a public bar would have been a sensation. I can't really imagine what would have happened.

. . . let there be no fear that this dynamic personality is likely to become no more than a lofty crag in a range of spent volcanoes. He is a national figure and will remain such.

## Michael Page

'The Don': the adored hero, almost demi-god, of the cricket field, against whom all other batsmen have been measured and found wanting.

The newspapers devoted more space to Bradman's illness than to that of any other person before or since except reigning monarchs, and the British public read the reports with an interest as anxious as if Bradman had been one of their own people.

## Michael Parkinson

My father went to his grave unrepentant. Retelling the story—as he did many times—he'd say, 'But I saw *him* bat and they didn't.'

## George Payne

He was a very good, quiet kid who never had much to say. Just a nice lad, no foolishness about him.

## Ian Peebles

The gates at Lord's closed early on the first morning, and it was clear that the chief attraction for this large crowd was Bradman.

### FRANK PERCY

*A knighthood has been bestowed on one of the finest sportsmen the world has ever known.*

### KEN PIESSE

Sir Donald Bradman remains cricket's most illustrious name . . . No Australian has rivalled his feats.

### L O S POIDEVIN

. . . no innings played by an Australian ever aroused such widespread popular interest.

### JACK POLLARD

*When he was not out by the luncheon interval, word spread like magic, and people kept arriving all through the break, pressing through to vantage points.*

Many women were among this new cricket audience, for it had become socially advantageous to have watched the great man.

He was mobbed in theatres and major stores, with women jostling each other to get close enough to kiss him.

Bradman's success was so complete, accomplished as it was in the land of our forebears, that it gave Australians a new sense of pride and proof that they were no longer second-rate.

### WILLIAM POLLOCK

Australia is Bradman mad; you hear his name all day long in the mouths of men, women and children.

London needs a bigger ground. Lord's is too small for a Bradman day.

And he is probably the greatest gate attraction cricket has ever known—a far greater money-spinner at the turnstiles than were W G, Ranji, Jack Hobbs.

There are fewer people in the whole of Australia than there are in London, and most of them idolise their little champion of cricket. And 'the Don' copes with it splendidly.

### 'THE REFEREE'

In Bradman, they have one of the most remarkable batsmen of all time, whose personality radiates optimism, keenness, and kindliness.

### 'REUTERS'

Cricket lost its Babe Ruth when Donald George Bradman, idol of Australia and terror of opposing teams, ended his first-class match career.

Few sportsmen ever received more honour and appreciation from their compatriots than Bradman did from his Australians.

### V Y RICHARDSON

This birth of 'Bradmanism' helped the Australians from 161 to 404 in 165 minutes . . .

### R C ROBERTSON-GLASGOW

No artist has more shrewdly understood and satisfied his public.

In the commerce of cricket he was the best salesman that the game has yet seen.

In a sense it was the spectators who made most of his runs. When he had scored 100 on his own, it was they that took it on to 200 or 300. They wanted records, and Bradman dressed his window accordingly.

### RAY ROBINSON

*On his debut at the age of 19 for NSW at Adelaide Oval his 118 was like the first rim of sun above the horizon.*

### IRVING ROSENWATER

Sydney forgot its dearer bread, the bitter struggle over the Banking Bill and that the New South Wales wheat crop was in jeopardy: all went to see Bradman.

No other touring cricketer has been so accepted—not Trumper, not Macartney, not George Headley, no one.

*King George and Queen Mary telephoned from Balmoral to send their wishes for his speedy recovery. It was the King's expressed desire that he be kept in constant touch with Bradman's progress. 'I want to know everything,' the King said.*
*(on Bradman's critical illness in 1934)*

The crowds were delirious with delight—more than 32 000 were watching—and after it was all over, there were some people who chose never to go to the Sydney Cricket

Ground again but who rested content with the imperishable memory of a brilliant innings by a brilliant man.

With typical national masochism, English crowds came back again and again to see him tear their bowlers to ribbons.

His return in triumph to his homeland was likened to a successful Roman general returning from the wars.

The lionising potential of Bradman was to manifest itself in due course in all sorts of things—Bradman shirts, bats, pads, boots, gloves, ties, shoes, hats, special drinks, dances, and even lolly sticks for children.

Those with perception could see that here was not only a cricket phenomenon but an administrative phenomenon too, for how many people would now be flocking to grounds to watch this batsman at work?

The Australian public by then certainly saw him as a greater attraction than ever. To them Bradman was king, to be hero-worshipped as no games player had ever been idolised before in Australia.

It is strange how the British public almost willed him to do well at the expense of their own cricketers, having accepted his genius since the early days of 1930 and never daring to suppose that the genius could dim.

Fame, deriving of course from his great skill, made Sir Donald Bradman one of the imperishable sporting figures of the twentieth century.

### ELZA SCHOLZ

*Don was always a good boy, and a bonny baby.*
*He was a sturdy little chap.*

### BRIAN SELLERS

He has given me and hundreds of thousands of others great pleasure during his wonderful career. Well played, Don!

### H SHEAFFE

Everybody throughout Australia and the Empire had followed the exploits of this young genius . . .

### SIR JOYNTON SMITH

He has won a place in the thoughts and affections of all classes of the community, which is but rarely achieved by prime ministers, or even monarchs who stand high in the regard of the people.

### SYDNEY SMITH JNR

. . . all those who know this brilliant boy are impressed by his striking modesty.

### SPECIAL REPRESENTATIVE

The English crowd has taken to Bradman as a gallery of flappers takes to a cinema idol . . .

### 'SUN'

Bradman's appearance is now easily the finest sight in cricket.

## 'SUN NEWS-PICTORIAL'

There will be no rise in bread prices while the Test cricket is on. A meeting of the Master Bakers Council that was to take place yesterday to consider an increase has been postponed until Thursday afternoon—if the cricket is finished by then. Members of the Council were unanimous that watching Bradman yesterday was more entertaining that risking the wrath of housewives by raising prices.

## 'SUSSEX DAILY NEWS'

The trouble with Don Bradman, of course, is that unless he scores a century in every innings the newspapers print sensational bills about him.

When he struck that bad patch shortly after the tour began, 'Bradman's Duck' was placarded up and down London in bigger type than if another war had been declared.

## E W SWANTON

The cricket world had never known such phenomenal scoring. . . . The Bradman legend was born that day.

Cricket is a batsman's game. The city of London has never emptied to watch a bowler as it did to watch Bradman.

## 'SYDNEY MORNING HERALD'

Bradman has been idolised for his maintained brilliance and his almost superhuman skill.

Every newspaper and every Englishman who has an interest in cricket is discussing the secret of Bradman's wizardry.

### GEOFFREY TEBUTT

The immense popularity of Don Bradman with the public was echoed among his team mates.

. . . but it was his youth, his romantic and meteoric rise to first-class rank, his utter imperturbability when confronting bowlers of world-wide renown, which caused him to become the most-talked-of man in England . . .

### A A THOMSON

> *As he left the crease after this, his last great innings at Headingley, the crowd rose to him, cheering and clapping until throats and palms were sore.*

From this summer came the beginning of the imperial sway which some enterprising journalist called Bradmanism.

Don Bradman, who was not only uncrowned king in Australia but cricket's emperor all over the world.

### F R TRUEMAN

. . . Don Bradman, most famous Aussie cricketer of all time.

### F H TYSON

The public, accustomed to the batting fireworks of his era, became listless at the mortal material served up to them as cricket.

*(on Bradman's retirement)*

## Unknown Newspaper

*The Bishops observed that there was a good deal
of swapping autographs going on among the
choirboys . . . 12 bishops' autographs were regu-
larly traded for one of Don Bradman's.*

## R B Vincent

A more certain run-maker he could not be expected to be,
but there is a self-pleasure, relieved of anxiety, in his batsmanship which makes him every bit as dear to an English
crowd as were Macartney and Trumper . . .

## Sir Pelham Warner

. . . and it is no exaggeration to say that not even W G—at
Bradman's age—had attained so world-wide a reputation.

## Percy Westbrook

We want to tell you we love you, Don, and are proud of
you. He is one of us.

He is worthy of all the praise lavished upon him, and no
one need fear its effect on his character, as he remains today
the same frank, open boy he was years ago.

So this wonder player captured the imagination and won the
affections of a vast multitude on the other side of the world ...

## Eric Whitehead

He becomes the first cricketer to slug his way to a
knighthood.

### R S WHITINGTON

> *Bradman was rarely happier than when in the company of children.*

Bradman brought colour, excitement, patriotic pride, escape from life lived day in and drab day out among depressing, factory-smut-blackened alleyways to millions of these people.

Don has known the roar of the crowd as few other cricketers have. It was his constant companion for the greater part of 23 years.

Sir Don's service to the people of the British Commonwealth has been incalculable even in titles.

How many members of the general, non-cricketing public have been attracted to the cricket grounds of England and Australia during the last 20 years purely to say they have seen the phenomenal Bradman?

### TREVOR WIGNALL

> *When Bradman exceeded Foster's record, the enthusiasm was so terrific that play had to be stopped until the noise diminished.*

### JIM WILSON

Biggest sports news for years is the knighthood conferred on Don Bradman.

### 'WISDEN CRICKETERS' ALMANACK'

It is not too much to say that he took both England and the whole cricket world by storm.

## N W D YARDLEY

I think the greatest pleasure Hedley [Verity] got in his whole life was bowling to Don Bradman.

For me, it is an honour and a pleasure to have played against him.

## YORKSHIREMAN

We do not come to see the Australians play, we joost come to see Bradman baht.

## THE CRAFTSMAN
### With No Edge to His Bat

*'Think of it—a brilliant batsman
with no edge to his bat and
who doesn't take a risk.'*

SIR NEVILLE CARDUS

37

### 'THE ADVERTISER'

He showed himself to be not only a stroke executor, but also a stroke manufacturer . . .

### G O ALLEN

He had two shots for every ball when he was going well.

### H S ALTHAM

The power and versatility of his stroke-play is astonishing.

He sees the ball sooner, watches it longer and can play the stroke later than anyone else.

Allied with this great variety of stroke-play there goes an extraordinary facility for placing the ball, and only very accurate bowling and the most skilfully adjusted placing of the field has any chance of keeping him even moderately quiet on a good wicket.

### JOHN ARLOTT

*Yet Bradman in 1948, forty years old, was still playing strokes impossible to any other cricketer in the world.*

This was the master batsman against all types of bowling and on all kinds of surfaces.

He would pull a ball quite unconcernedly and with such certainty that it seemed his eye was flawless and the bat an extension of his arm . . .

Bradman was the nearest thing in batting to infallibility—but it was human, not inhuman infallibility.

He undoubtedly had an extra gift of perception; an ability to see and assess the curve, length and pace of the ball earlier than any other player we have ever seen.

### E W BALLENTINE

His strokes radiated beautifully round the wicket like the spokes of a cartwheel.

### ERIC BARBOUR

There was no trace of wildness in Bradman's hitting. It was an instance of sheer resolution and machine-like steadiness.

### RALPH BARKER

The power and certainty of Bradman's stroke-play were exhilarating. His wonderful eye, quick footwork, and supple, powerful wrists put him in a class by himself at forcing the good-length ball to the boundary.

### S G BARNES

The game took on another flavour when Bradman was batting and I knew I had something to learn in the game. Bradman was the one who could teach me.

### DENZIL BATCHELOR

*It did not seem to matter who was in with him, or what was bowled to him—he was the text-book batsman, with a pat answer to every problem.*

But a long innings by Bradman leaves one's critical sense dazzled. The game has suddenly become absurdly easy.

### A V BEDSER

His placements amounted to an exact science.

Bradman's defensive bat was as straight as it could be—almost puritanically orthodox.

I cannot accept that there was anything in batting technique beyond him.

### A J BELL

Most people in South Africa seem to be under the impression that Bradman is a great forward player. This is quite erroneous. He is the finest back player any of us have ever seen.

His command of shots is nothing short of marvellous. He seems to know just what kind of ball you are going to bowl and where you are going to bowl it.

### W E BOWES

I never saw him bat on a 'sticky-dog' but I did see him on a pitch where the ball was turning and you couldn't get the ball past his bat.

### GEORGE BRADMAN *(father)*

At the age of eight or nine he was a very fair bat.

### 'BRITISH WEEKLY'

*One shot, among many, lingers in the memory most bewitchingly. One ball looked like hitting his boot—a 'Yorker' from the Yorkshire son of Anak, Bowes; then, hey presto! the feet twinkled, stepped a pace back; bat and ball were in perfectly timed contact, and lo! the ball was in the crowd in the twinkling of an eye!*

## F R BROWN

'The Don' proceeded to make a magnificent 71 out of a total of 128 on a 'sticky'. I don't recall him giving the vestige of a chance; and not unnaturally I am inclined to be sceptical when I hear tales that Bradman was a broken reed in these conditions.

He always seemed to have just that extra time to play the ball but, to my mind, the outstanding thing about his play was his uncanny placing between the fielders.

## SIR NEVILLE CARDUS

*I suppose no man has ever been more of a master of his job than Bradman is master of his job. He is as good a batsman as Bach was as a composer.*

The animal spirits in Bradman are never likely to go mad. He is a purist in a hurry: he administers the orthodox in long and apostolic knocks.

. . . and Bradman, in little more than two hours and a half had made 155, not once exerting himself, every shot dead in the target's middle, precise and shattering; an innings which was beautiful and yet somehow cruel in its excessive mastery.

It was all done without the turn of a hair—easy as Menuhin on his violin.

He changed batsmanship into an exact science, but a science with a difference; he dwarfed precedent and known values.

There were not enough fieldsmen available; Bradman found gaps and vacancies in nature.

He didn't move until the ball was on him; then the brilliant technique shot forth concentrated energy—and the axe fell.

Every fine point of batsmanship was to be admired, strokes powerful and swift and handsome; variety of craft controlled by singleness of mind and purpose.

His batsmanship delights one's knowledge of the game; his every stroke is a dazzling and precious stone in the game's crown.

He was, if we may abuse language, a 'deus ex machina'.

He could not make a hazardous flight; he reminded me of the trapeze performer who one night decided to commit suicide by flinging himself headlong to the stage but could not achieve the error because his skill had become so infallible . . .

### CLIFF CARY

Footwork is the basis of Bradman's triumphs. He learnt that without balance stroking was impossible. His fluency rested on the fact that he was in position for every shot he attempted.

### A P F CHAPMAN

*If Bradman had been fit to bat on this pitch, no bowler in the world could have got him out for less than 1000 runs.*

### D C S COMPTON

No single player, I can imagine it being said, could have been so impossibly gifted, or endowed with a temperament to match his extravagant ability.

Apart from his wonderful repertoire of strokes, Bradman's outstanding quality, in my opinion, is an ability to memorise the placing of the field.

Once he goes to the crease Don Bradman forgets everything else but the scoring of runs.

### GERRY COTTER

He was the most superbly organised batsman the game has known, a man who allied perfect technique and the ability to play any stroke to any ball with limitless concentration, an abundance of self-confidence and an insatiable desire both to score runs and to win.

### 'COUNTRY LIFE'

He is a master at moving quietly and smoothly out to the pitch, and it is almost impossible to bowl a length to him.

### M C COWDREY

He came nearer to mastering the art of batsmanship than anyone. He had astonishing fleetness of foot, sharpness of eye and timing, but it was his mind that powered his success.

### ROBERT CRADDOCK

Asking someone to list Bradman's array of strokes is like trying to name all of the Beatles' top hits. There was the textbook and more.

### 'CRICKETER'

His cricket went along its manifold ways with a security which denied its own brilliance.

### 'DAILY CHRONICLE'

For fluency of stroke-play Bradman is perfection, the beauty being that he uses his bat as a weapon of offence.

### 'DAILY EXPRESS'

Bradman's innings was a masterpiece of calm and concise cricket.

### 'DAILY HERALD'

Bradman's innings brought gladness to the heart of the cricketer and cricket lovers not merely for its record breaking, but for things almanacs do not mention, courage and craftsmanship.

### 'DAILY PICTORIAL'

It is quite possible that Bradman will prove to be the finest run-getting machine ever known, and as a stylist he improves at each appearance.

### KEN DALBY

Bradman, however, scaled once more the Olympian heights of glory to complete a faultless century . . .

### PHILIP DERRIMAN
*(quoting Bill O'Reilly)*

*Even in the cradle Don Bradman wouldn't have done anything that wasn't thought out.*

### E R DEXTER

. . . the swing of the bat, the end of the bat pointing upwards, well above his hands, a lovely shoulder position, immaculate footwork, everything in the right place at the right time.

### E W DOCKER

> *Move a man from one spot and he was sure to hit the next ball through that very spot. He had a photographic memory for this sort of thing.*

. . . he had acquired the ability to play two or more shots off the same delivery, making it just impossible for the bowler to set a field for him.

Bradman just went on and on, remorselessly. There seemed no reason why he should ever get out; no means of containing him at all.

### SIDNEY DOWNER

. . . a phenomenal example of self-control, patience, and his own matchless brand of skilled batsmanship.

He has all the strokes known to man and many others known only to himself.

He can retreat towards the square-leg umpire and hit the fastest bowler of a generation past cover for four, he can run out of his ground to drive spin, change his mind and back-cut it against the break. All this and the heaven to which only Bradman can aspire . . .

### L B DUCKWORTH

> *. . . but I have never seen any other batsman who looked as if he could do whatever he pleased with any ball sent down to him—and usually did.*

Those who saw Larwood and Voce bowling at their fastest will have some glimmering of the difficulty of such strokes. I can think of no other batsman who could even have attempted them.

### ELTON EDE

Bradman's mastery and reserve power is comparable with a great singer, and his achievement is equally satisfying.

### H V EVATT

But the outstanding quality of his batting skill is that he employs it functionally, ever adjusting it to the task at hand.

Whatever the original limitations of his stroke repertoire, Bradman has become the master of every stroke in the game.

### KENNETH FARNES

His technical efficiency is astounding, as a box-office attraction he is supreme . . .

### G A FAULKNER

It is not possible to imagine a more workmanlike innings than that given us by this great little Australian. The young man is a cricket phenomenon.

He possesses a remarkably quick brain; he knows immediately what, and where, the ball is; he allows the ball to get right under him before playing at it; and he rejoices in a mental make-up which combines the alertness of youth with the stability of middle age. His judgement is decisive; his movements definite.

### P G H FENDER

As perfect an example of real batting, in its best sense, as anyone could wish to see.

Bradman's batting was an education in itself . . .

Until we saw Bradman this summer, I do not think that any of us realised that it was possible to be so really brilliant without taking risks.

### W H FERGUSON

Leeds, 1930, will always be Bradman's match of matches: all else pales into insignificance when placed alongside Don's incredible knock.

### J H FINGLETON

*He was the best in making the placement of a field look foolish.*

He made it all look so easy, so simple, so prearranged.

His superb judgement, his swift and unerring footwork down the pitch gave few bowlers an appetite for the job against him and they realised there was no such thing as a good length to him.

The position of his left hand by no means explains the secret of his pull stroke. His footwork in this stroke was absolutely faultless—nay, miraculous.

### C B FRY

*I wish I could have used my bat like Don. He's a gem of a batsman. I just love his finished technique and inevitable surety. How he must enjoy getting his runs.*

## T W GRAVENEY

Along with all his polished batting skills he also had the vital
ingredient that you will find in the cocktail that goes to
make any great batsman—the ability to give total
concentration to the job of scoring the next run.

## BENNY GREEN

It was instantly apparent that Bradman, with his virtually
flawless technique and limitless powers of concentration, was
about to debase the coinage of run-making as nobody
before him, that he was technically equipped and
temperamentally inclined to go on batting forever.

## I GUPTA

Bradman provided my players with their greatest cricket
show.

## F J C GUSTARD

Though he keeps the ball almost invariably on the ground,
he has been known to hit sixes, and his supreme confidence
completes the make-up of a wonderful batting genius.

## W R HAMMOND

Any batsman who can affect field settings, as Bradman and
Ponsford have done, is among the truly great.

## R N HARVEY

*There is nothing he doesn't know about cricket
and no matter how long a player has been in the
game an hour's chat with Sir Donald will teach
him more about the intricacies of batting and
bowling than he ever dreamed of.*

### V S HAZARE

The shrewd player that he was he knew what was happening and when the first ball was bowled outside the off-stump it was promptly swept to the square-leg boundary.

He had more than one stroke for the same ball and hence it became very difficult to set the correct field for him and to check his flow of runs.

### GEORGE HELE

I have watched no batsman of any era so completely in control of an attack. This was one of the greatest innings, in a technical sense, that I have umpired for, or seen.

Don was to batting almost what Walter Lindrum was to billiards. Applying the precision Lindrum employed, he used to score threes from the last balls of overs, not singles, to retain the strike.

### H J HENLEY

He seems to have every stroke in the cricket book, from the long-handled drive to the short-armed hook, and he revives the almost lost art of the late cut.

### C HILL

. . . characteristic Bradman, hardly a flaw, with his usual perfect footwork and timing so full of snap.

### SIR JACK HOBBS

My candid opinion of Bradman? Well, it is this. He is the best batsman in the world on dry wickets, and probably on all wickets if given the opportunity to get used to wet ones.

I am satisfied that only leg theory can stop Bradman. The power that he gets in his strokes, and their very wide range alike, are wonderful. He hits freely where others just defend.

## GERALD HOWAT

In his three massive innings he totalled 651 runs in 18½ hours without giving a chance. The whole enterprise had been a triumph of willpower, decision-making and technical skill.

## SIR LEN HUTTON

I found him as sound technically, as any player I have yet seen.

His movements were so right and so emphatic.

He must have memorised the exact position of every fielder to an inch, and his movements at the crease were precise and quick and ending in perfect position to make the stroke of his choice.

He could pull the ball exactly where he wanted it to go—and that is no exaggeration.

## R ILLINGWORTH/KENNETH GREGORY

Bradman was playing as correctly as H L Collins sober to produce results which would never for one moment have been contemplated by H L Collins drunk.

## PETER JACKSON

Although two successive deliveries may have been almost identical, that did not mean they would be hit in the same direction.

### C L R JAMES

The thing that strikes me—and I have seen Sir Donald play many times and make many hundreds of runs—is the scientific, systematic manner in which he analyses the danger.

### I W JOHNSON

Often, however, he would unleash a stroke the like of which had never been seen before. This was not so much a case of unorthodoxy as his ability to produce what nobody else had thought about, let alone tried.

Don was the complete batsman.

### JAMES A JONES

We look at Bradman with something like despair. He is a beautiful craftsman we know . . .

He is like a robot. Runs come to him as though they were being manufactured by a slow but infinitely efficient machine. And though the Englishmen crouch around like panthers, they seem powerless to stop this implacable progress . . .

### L H KEARNEY

*He played such a multiplicity of strokes that there were too many positions made for eleven Indian fieldsmen to fill.*

### BEN KERVILLE

His rigid self-control, his life-time of devotion to the mastery of his subject, and the great sacrifices that were necessary to follow such a straight and narrow devotional line were beyond the capacity of his fellows.

### J M KILBURN

No other batsman matched his capacity for avoiding error without falling into immobility.

. . . he has carried the cricket of his time to ultimate efficiency.

### J C LAKER

*As I ran up, Bradman seemed to know what I was going to bowl, where the ball was going to pitch, and how many runs he was going to score. That was exactly the uncanny impression he gave.*

### P K LEE

Don played many fine innings in his life. But it's that first one that really sticks in my mind.

### TONY LEWIS

Bradman thought about batting and was able to put his theories into voracious practice.

### PHILIP LINDSAY

*Far from mechanical, Bradman's batting that day was inhuman only because it was chanceless. Nor was it just that dogged chancelessness of a bore who will take no risks; he took what to an ordinary mortal would have been risks enough to stop one's heart, only one's heart missed no beat because here was Bradman at work, Apollo on earth, and one knew that he could not fail.*

Machine, indeed! Show me a machine that can drive and cut and glance so merrily, with that brisk footwork, that saucy contempt for any devilishness the bowler might think to put with burning fingers in the ball.

## C G MACARTNEY

He is the supreme test for bowlers, and nothing yet devised by spin or swing, pace or slowness, seems to provide any unpleasant moment for him.

## G F McCLEARY

As one notes what the Don's bat does to the ball one wonders why he ever gets out.

All his strokes are a delight to the eye, but perhaps the most fascinating is the late cut; he plays the ball as if he loves it and is sending it to the boundary for its own good.

It is not necessary to be a cricketer to realise as the Don takes his place at the wicket that he is a man who knows his job. You have the same feeling when Toscanini walks onto the platform.

## ALAN McGILVRAY

Like Al Jolson, a popular American singer of the time, he had come back more mellow, his art refined and seasoned and richer in character.

## A C MacLAREN

It was sometimes possible to get Macartney out by inciting him early to play a characteristic stroke, which nobody else would attempt, but Bradman never allows himself any liberty.

### A A MAILEY

How to get Bradman out is developing into a pastime for rainy days.

### L V MANNING

When Bradman scores fast he does it without hurrying. He accelerates without any apparent physical effort. Above all he makes no mistake.

### JOHN MARSHALL

Nor will those present forget the majestic 133 not out scored by Bradman—his last innings at Old Trafford which was suitably, emotionally, acclaimed.

### G D MARTINEAU

He learnt to bat under the crudest conditions, in a backyard, and developed, with little coaching or advice, into what has been called the greatest run-getting machine the world has ever known.

### RONALD MASON

. . . trustworthy judges beside think this score of 254 to be the most masterly of all his great innings: in intent and perfection of execution it was flawless, and it established him without any manner of doubt as the greatest batsman then playing.

*(Bradman's Test innings at Lord's in 1930)*

Predictable enough, yes: but what was the use when he was apparently impregnable too?

I am prepared to believe that any shot made by Bradman had a better chance of succeeding in its object than any shot made by anyone else . . .

## JIM MATHERS

Bradman is generalissimo of stroke equipment.

## SIR ROBERT MENZIES

The immense authority of his batting, the complete justice with which he dealt with each ball on its merits and despatched it on what seemed to be its predestined errand have made him the undisputed master batsman of my time.

## K R MILLER

*When he hooked the ball he could almost choose the picket it was going to hit along the boundary.*

He controlled his hook-shot as I have never seen any other batsman control it.

## P J MOSS

It seems obvious, yet shift a man from a place in the field and I'll wager Bradman finds the gap.

## A G MOYES

*He could beat the field, get runs off nearly every ball and in so doing perplex the bowler, weary the fieldsmen, and drive the opposing captain frantic in his effort to stop the stream of runs.*

If we get back to first principles, the scoring of runs, there cannot be much doubt where Bradman stands in cricket. It is impossible to place anyone ahead of him.

No player who ever lived has had more time to make his stroke than Bradman.

The plain fact is that Bradman can score a century before lunch or 300 in a day and then so turn his game upside down and conquer his ambitions that for hour after hour he becomes deaf to everything but the ticking of the clock.

His 334 at Leeds was a masterpiece of skill, a revelation of supreme artistry.

### PATRICK MURPHY

His orderly mind played a vital role in his batting. He treated it like a business, something to be approached with dedication and professionalism.

Bradman brought to his batting a strength of mind and purpose that was rock-solid and pitiless.

### 'NOT OUT'

His high scoring, his precision in timing and placing, and the selection of stroke for any particular ball, is taking on the guise of the mechanical.

### 'OBSERVER'

Bradman's innings was a marvellous display of clever, stylish and almost faultless batting. The most ardent Surrey partisan could not grudge any of his runs. Recollection of the innings will always be happy to those privileged to witness it.

### W A OLDFIELD

It was classic in every respect and the great crowds who saw it will never forget the brilliance of his stroke-play, due to his audacious footwork, the quickness of his eye, and his supreme confidence.

His development of stroke-play and self-control as he progressed in the game was to me amazing.

### W J O'REILLY

In all Bradman's career, and I have seen a great deal of it, I have never known him to be guilty of falling into the same trap twice.

To have him on my side meant two things. Firstly, I would not be facing the job of bowling at him. Secondly, he usually scored enough runs to make my bowling job easy.

### MICHAEL PAGE

Bradman was universally recognised as the greatest player of the hook shot and pull shot that cricket has ever known.

Allen, Tate, White, Robins and Hammond alternated in efforts to dismiss him, but his brilliant footwork and unerring eyes defeated them every time.

### JOHN PARKER

*He had a reputation for ruthlessness, but that wasn't really deserved. His attitude was simply perfectionist.*

### L O S POIDEVIN

There is nothing complicated, for instance, in Don Bradman's batting technique, it is just the simple things of batsmanship done to perfection and repeated *ad infinitum*.

The grandeur of his batting does not show itself in any particular stroke or even set of strokes, but in their successful placement.

## JACK POLLARD

He turned batting into a precise art as he punished all bowlers with an almost arrogant confidence.

No batsman has hit the ball along the ground as consistently as Bradman and there have been few better runners between the wickets.

Two-thirds of his first-class centuries were chanceless and he seldom lofted the ball until his team was dominating a match.

## DANIEL REESE

Cricket could never be a dull game when Bradman was batting. Although Bradman has a wide range of strokes it is mainly his placing that enables him to score at such speed.

## W RHODES

He has so many shots—every one of them—he is so sharp at judging the length of a ball, and, what is more, he can place the ball with such astonishing accuracy.

He makes the bowling suit his batting—which is real cricket and the right spirit of cricket.

## V Y RICHARDSON

What made him so great as a batsman were, I think:
- tremendous co-ordination between eye and mind;
- extraordinary quickness and correctness of footwork;
- the ability to gauge the quality and nature of a ball almost immediately it left a bowler's hand;
- his phenomenal concentration and apparently unlimited stamina;
- his sheer delight in scoring runs and conquering bowlers;
- his insatiable ambition.

## R C Robertson-Glasgow

> *About his batting there was to be no style for style's sake . . . his aim was the making of runs, and he made them in staggering and ceaseless profusion.*

In the popular view, Bradman is the batsman of colossal scores, a machine that turns out runs as other machines turn out screws or sausages.

So, the machine prevailed, but the artist was there just the same, that wonderful combination of eye, wrist, foot, and judgement . . .

He seemed to have eliminated error, to have perfected the mechanism of stroke.

## Ray Robinson

Bradman's unrivalled skill normally allowed him to do almost as he liked.

To understand him properly, you have to get down from the peaks to the lower levels of his career. Chief result of this mountaineering is to heighten the wonder of his deeds and to discover that he is an even more remarkable batsman than is commonly thought.

Many great batsmen have had the faculty of changing the stroke, but none in my time has done it as often as Bradman did on his last tour of Britain.

Gap-finding shots hurried him along the trail, leaving barrackers howling for more, bowlers gasping for air and the turnstiles squeaking for oil.

## C F ROOT

There is no temerity about Bradman's methods. He does not suspect a trap in a half-volley, long hop, or full toss, and his method of defence is to attack.

## IRVING ROSENWATER

What Bradman did at Lord's can be summed up—but not exactly dismissed—in a single phrase: he played the most perfect innings of his life.

. . . a quite brilliant 254, renowned by no means simply for its numerical size but for the sheer perfection of its stroke-play and footwork. Not a chance was given; hardly a false stroke was made; never once was the ball lifted off the ground. That such perfection should have been maintained over a period of more than five and a half hours showed Bradman to possess not only a buoyant faith in himself but the most remarkable qualities of concentration and single-mindedness.

His limitless stroke range and power produced runs on a scale that the great stylists could not match.

Some bowlers were sure that he could even see the way the ball was spinning as it came through the air.

## BRIAN SELLERS

What struck me most of all was the ease with which he got his runs. At no time did he appear in difficulties. His footwork and stroke-play were perfect.

## E H D SEWELL

In the second Test he had made over 200 runs and in the third Test 153 before he raised a ball.

Bradman's strong points, ignoring his eye and obviously natural aptitude for, I guess, any ball game, are his timing, his refusal to be bound by any such silly fetish as not hitting a half volley because it happens to be early in his innings, and his ability to play forward powerfully.

### J SMITH

*Set a field for Bradman? Twenty-two men would not have been enough to plug all the holes he found in our run-saving barbed-wire entanglements during his masterpiece.*

### PETER SMITH

The most clinically efficient run-getter in cricket history.

### 'SMITHS WEEKLY'

And in came Bradman to set before the King as dainty a dish of batsmanship as has been seen throughout the last 20 years of international cricket.

### REGGIE SPOONER

We all pay tribute to his masterly skill.

### 'SPORTING LIFE'

He is a workman of the highest class, first, last, and all the time.

### K R STACKPOLE

*Bradman, of course, was in a category of his own; the one player who came close to mastering the game.*

What they must remember is that they can't hope to play every shot in the book. There's probably been only one fellow who could do that—Bradman.

### 'SUN SPECIAL'

It was a magnificent innings, a mixture of doggedness and audacity . . .

Bradman's 191 again emphasises his astonishing brilliance. The fact that all his performances have been achieved on rain-damaged wickets gives a touch of genius to his work.

### E W SWANTON

Bat and man seemed one, the ball persuaded by a marvellous precision of timing.

One sees in memory an endless succession of delicate cuts and deflections, hooks, indeed, strokes all round the compass, as length and direction dictated.

The impression that remains is of the smooth, unhurried rhythm of his play.

### GEOFFREY TEBBUTT

I have seen him score a good many hundreds in his many thousands of runs by strokes of delicacy which a billiardist may envy.

## LORD TENNYSON

I make bold to say that Bradman has all the strokes, and then some. He is competent to play any game—the game that, in its dash and gusto, is typically Bradmanesque, or one that tells of the scholar.

## GEORGE THATCHER

Batting looks ridiculously easy when Bradman is at work. He strings the runs together with the ease of an expert billiardist.

## A A THOMSON

*And in Bowral, a small sun-dried town some 80 miles south of Sydney, a boy of seven was throwing a golf ball at the brick stand supporting a big water-tank and hitting it as it came back with a small cricket stump. Cricket goes on.*

If he found himself guilty of a bad stroke, he would cut it surgically out of his repertory as a specialist might cut out a gangrene.

To those who say that Bradman was a mere run-getting machine, I would reply that this is the age of the beautiful machine and that no machine was more nearly perfect.

## 'THE TIMES'

A field cannot be set to such genius with the ability, in the twinkling of an eye, to find the exact stroke to any chosen part he may select . . .

To have seen Bradman at the wicket is to have enjoyed the precision of the art of batting.

Bradman has consistently scored from the deliveries which the majority of batsmen would be content to keep out of the wicket.

If he fails, Australia crashes.

It was in fact an innings so glorious that it might well be classed as incomparable, and how the Yorkshiremen loved it.

. . . for yesterday we were privileged once again to see the batsman who is the complete proof that a bowler can bowl only so well as the striker allows him to do.

### H TRUMBLE

Don Bradman must be classed as the batsman of today. He evidently possesses a cricket brain, and his wonderful eye and footwork make him a brilliant exponent of all strokes.

### H VERITY

Don't ever tell me that Don is just ordinary on the sticky ones.

It was a pig of a pitch and he played me in the middle of the bat right through.

### R B VINCENT

*. . . for sheer and continual efficiency his performances are truly astounding.*

To describe his strokes would be impossible. He hit the ball in every conceivable corner of the field.

. . . a display of batsmanship which in ease of scoring combined with absolute security could not be surpassed.

There is a certitude in his batsmanship, mental as well as technical, which I cannot believe has belonged to any other cricketer since W G . . .

### B J WAKLEY

With the defence of a stone-waller, beautiful footwork, perfect technique, and as many brilliant and powerful strokes as any hitter, he also displayed immense gifts of judgement, concentration, temperament and stamina.

### PAT WARD-THOMAS

Perhaps less often than any other great batsman did he hit the ball in the air, in his merciless fashion giving the fielders the least possible chance.

### SIR PELHAM WARNER

An idealism which urged him to learn everything he possibly could, and to profit by the lessons learnt.

England must evolve a new type of bowler, and develop fresh ideas, strategy and tactics, to curb his almost uncanny skill.

. . . that bowling to Bradman was like throwing stones at the Rock of Gibraltar.

His cutting was superb, he drove with great power, and any ball the least short was hooked always along the ground. It was the great man at his greatest.

## C WASHBROOK

*While the bowler was walking back to his starting point, Don would run his eye round the off-side fieldsmen, starting from gully, right to mid-off and then to the bowler. By this method, which he appeared to employ before every ball, he carried in his mind a clear picture of where every off-side fieldsman was situated.*

. . . and no matter how fast the bowler against him, he was in a position to play his strokes so easily that he always looked to be waiting for the ball to reach him.

## R S WHITINGTON

He developed his innings as the great billiard player, Walter Lindrum, developed his mammoth breaks . . .

He took to his cricket a degree of scientific concentration, application and ambition that few men in any field of activity have equalled.

## TREVOR WIGNALL

It is doubtful whether any cricketer in the world has ever played a greater, more technically perfect, and more memorable innings. It was flawless, and deserves the description 'magnificent' because of the variety of strokes displayed.

### 'WISDEN CRICKETERS' ALMANACK'

*An amazingly brilliant batsman, he retained that faculty, given to most really great players, of delaying his stroke until the last possible moment.*

He can turn to leg, and cut with delightful accuracy but above all he is a superb driver.

He hit very hard in front of the wicket, scored splendidly on the leg side and very often cut in dazzling fashion.

In 1930 English crowds saw for the first time the art of infallible batsmanship and on a good wicket raised to unprecedented heights by the mastery of the young Bradman.

A glorious driver, he hit the ball very hard, while his placing was almost invariably perfect.

As usual, he rarely lifted the ball and when making two or more consecutive scoring strokes seldom sent it in the same direction.

. . . Bradman, in putting together the highest innings played for Australia in any Test match in that country, showed that exceptional combination of skill and judgement that has produced from him so many triumphs.

### R E S WYATT

He was a run-getting machine whose like had never been seen before.

## N W D YARDLEY

No one could have played better—wonderful footwork, immaculate defence and impeccable stroke selection.

## 'YORKSHIRE POST'

The methods of this sane and normal genius, confirmed by the almost miraculous scores he makes, are likely to improve both batting and bowling, and his influence may be felt for a generation.

SATURDAY JULY 12

BRADMAN
VERSUS
ENGLAND

## THE WARRIOR
### The World versus Bradman

'*In the 20 years of the Australian's
reign it became the habit
to think of cricket as a question of
the World v Bradman.*'

**A A THOMSON**

69

## WALTER ALLEN

> *A S MacLaren . . . 'Yes, I know he's pretty good,*
> *but he's got a lot to learn.'*
> *Walter Allen . . . 'Look here, Archie, if he learns*
> *much more, he will ruin the game.'*

## H S ALTHAM

Dictators are the order of the day, but neither Duce nor Fuhrer has dominated his own sphere more completely or more dramatically than Don Bradman has his.

## L AMARNATH

Bradman was the master yesterday. We did our best and I thought we did very well, too—but Don was magnificent.

## L E G AMES

All of the MCC's great players agreed Bradman would be one of the mainstays of Australian cricket for years, but none I am sure visualised that the serious-faced 'Boy from Bowral' would become the greatest menace English cricket had ever had.

## JOHN ARLOTT

He never knew a real spell of failure, but his successes were monumental.

Bradman has passed over the fields of England like a steam-roller.

## 'THE AUSTRALIAN CRICKETER'

Don has proved himself to be a cricketer without nerves and was gifted with a supreme confidence in his ability to learn and master bowlers.

### T E BAILEY

*'The Don' was unique, a young god, who played with mere mortals.*

### E H M BAILLIE

He began his career with a century and has been making centuries ever since.

. . . he never flattered the bowler with the faintest suggestion that they would ever get him out.

### E W BALLENTINE

Is there any limit to the scoring powers of this human machine?

### S F BARNES

Well, I won't say I couldn't have got him out at my best, but I would have needed to be at my very best.

### DENZIL BATCHELOR

But the salient impression that Bradman's innings gave, during its six infallible hours, was that it was beyond human power to get him out.

The fast bowlers at their fastest and most refreshed were powerless against him.

### A J BELL

The remarkable thing about the little wizard is that while fast and medium bowling is fresh he contents himself by never attempting to score in front of the wicket . . .

We tried for four and a half months to get him caught in the slips.

He has done enough to make 20 average men swollen-headed. And yet that is the last thing one could accuse him of.

### BEN BENNISON

A more serious young man or one richer in power of concentration I have not met. He did not play cricket for the mere joy of playing cricket. Cricket was his profession, and his unswerving purpose was to reach the top.

### SIR WILLIAM NORMAN BIRKETT

. . . the great figure of Bradman dominates the scene as he dominated the field on his last tour of this country.

### B J T BOSENQUET

*What a difference when Bradman came—'vin ordinaire' at one end and champagne at the other.*

### W E BOWES

. . . he just toyed with the field.

We used to win the odd psychological battle against Don, but he was a far better batsman than I was a bowler . . .

### GEORGE BRADMAN *(father)*

*His enthusiasm, grit and determination, coupled with the right temperament, have carried him through.*

### JOHN BRIGHT

Bradman, though the critics said he was stale, made a glorious 232.

### 'BRITISH WEEKLY'

And so hour after hour went by and one wondered if that lissom figure could ever get out.

### GERALD BRODRIBB

Bradman was another who in his early cricketing years had to rely on his own resources and unfaltering determination.

### F R BROWN

*Primarily, then, body-line was worked out as a weapon to put a curb on Bradman's mammoth scoring.*

### FRANK BROWNE

Bradman tamed tigers for nobody.

'The Don' had swept through England in the summer of 1930, with an effect on the cricketing inhabitants which could only be compared to that created by William the Conqueror, on the Saxons.

The idol was back on his pedestal, serene and terrible . . .

### SIR NEVILLE CARDUS

*A number of Bradmans would quickly put an end to the glorious uncertainty of cricket.*

The advent of Bradman on this Saturday of burning English summer was like the throwing of combustible stuff on fires that had been slumbering with dreadful potentiality.

Not by Bradman is the fancy made to roam; he is, for me, a batsman living, moving, and having his being wholly in cricket.

The latest innings by him had a plan and an executive skill which were terrifying.

Bradman's innings acquired a preposterous immensity. The ruthlessness of it all! First a long critical inspection of the opposition, each bowler weighed in the balance as though by codified law. Then, as soon as he had put everybody into a class—and worn them out by keeping them in suspense— he made fools of their pretensions to skill.

### HARRY CARSON

The whole of these Test matches centre on Bradman, and the general opinion is that if we cannot get him out in three overs we may have to wait three days.

### CLIF CARY

He accomplished much that was great. His feats will never be approached . . . Bradman was truly a wrecker but also a batsman whose name will live forever.

### A P F CHAPMAN

*As for Bradman, I hope he gets housemaid's knee before the next Test.*

This brilliant batsman is too good for us. He has never looked like getting out.

## D C S Compton

He gathered runs at such speed that it was impossible to set a field for him, and it occurred to me at times that he had a private game with a slow-moving fielder or with the opposing captain.

## 'Cricketer'

It has been generally agreed that, so far as results show, he was the most voracious run-getter and most consistent scourge of bowlers that the first-class game has ever experienced.

## 'Daily Telegraph'

Bradman dominated play as no one ever dominated in Test cricket before.

## Ken Dalby

Who was to bowl out the unbowlable Woodfull, shackle the prolific Ponsford, and then earn a knighthood by discovering some new Law of Motion to retard the phenomenal Bradman . . .

## H A De Lacy

Then he unfolded all his old genius as he allowed run-chasing to blossom into supremacy.

## E W DOCKER

*Before Bradman English cricket had been full of leg-traps and silly-mid-offs, inner and outer rings and all sorts of theoretical claptrap for containing the batsman, and the young Australian despatched the lot of them straight back to the pavilion where they belonged.*

## CHRISTOPHER DOUGLAS

Just when English cricket had regained its rightful position after the ignominies of the early twenties, Bradman had come along and upset everything.

## SIDNEY DOWNER

Yet, within this country boy, there lay a swift intelligence which the years sharpened into a wit capable of challenging and overthrowing the best-prepared ambiguities of forensic skill.

Bradman's cricket was of a different temper; it was the child of his mind.

## LOUIS DRUFFUS

Two or three more batsmen like Bradman in the world and the game of cricket would be ruined.

## W J EDRICH

. . . all England feels that now, at last, we may be able to fight for the Ashes on more equal terms again.

*(on Bradman's retirement)*

### T G EVANS

When once he was set, it was heart-breaking for bowlers and fielders.

### H V EVATT

Bradman's powers include, but are not limited to, magnificent batting skills, backed by patience, concentration and determination.

Indeed, the team value of this mammoth scores has been immense. His innings have ensured not only practical freedom from the risk of defeat, but very often actual victory.

### KENNETH FARNES

*The significant thing about his fantastic ability is that he never fails when his team has half a chance to win.*

### G A FAULKNER

His tenacity of purpose and machine-like precision astonish one.

### P G H FENDER

He seems to live for the exuberance of the moment.

### W H FERGUSON

On to Leeds, where in my opinion, Donald Bradman exceeded anything he had done previously, although, at the time, such a thing seemed impossible.

Not for Sir Donald the blackboard approach to the intricacies of batting. He was, above all, a natural cricketer, doing everything instinctively . . .

If he reached his century, he went after his 200, but even a double century he never regarded as an excuse for relaxation; it was merely another milepost on the road to 300.

## J H FINGLETON

### *To bat with him was an exercise in embarrassing futility.*

When he made a century, he made himself comfortable and settled down for two; when he had made 200 he cocked an eye for three, and if, by pushing himself a little further, it meant pushing somebody off a record pedestal, then, hey presto! Bradman called upon his superabundance of energy and magnificent concentration.

'The Don' was just too supreme and anybody who saw him bat would scoff at the suggestion that modern captaincy is now so gifted it would have nobbled him.

One does well to try and analyse Bradman's mind because, in all cricket, I met no other like it.

When you boiled Bradman down, when you analysed his eyesight, his footwork, his judgement, his range of strokes, there was still something left in which he was also superior to all others, and that was consistency.

## C B FRY

Don Bradman is a monopoly. Drama is afield the moment this jaunty dignity and purposeful poise emerge from the pavilion.

## A G Gardiner

He can make any team of crocks formidable against any challenge. So long as there is someone left to keep the other wicket intact, no game is so hopeless that he cannot snatch victory out of the jaws of defeat.

It was said of General Kleber that merely to look on him made men brave, and in the same way Bradman's presence in a team gives it the spirit of victory.

## Tom Garrett

Bradman's is a most marvellous feat—the best I ever knew. In fact, his whole performances are superior to those of any player ever sent from here.

## Alan Gibson

Through the thirties, if Australia were in any kind of trouble, and provided that it was a wicket which he felt he could play on, Bradman would score a couple of hundred to put them right.

. . . I think Englishmen should long have recognised that Bradman was the best of all batsmen . . .

## Maurice Golesworthy

Bradman was a veritable scoring machine, a cold and calculating record maker whose powers of endurance and sheer genius were almost inhuman.

## T W GRAVENEY

Don Bradman was past his peak by the time of the 1948 tour, but he was held in such awe that bowlers were intimidated by his very presence at the wicket.

He had a self-confidence that was quite chilling and there was not a bowler he did not feel he could master.

## BENNY GREEN

Bradman was now 22 years old, and patently a scourge for the England bowlers for years, perhaps decades, to come.

## 'GUARDIAN'

He plays so many grand innings, each of which seems more brilliant than the last, that it is difficult to pronounce which is his really greatest feat.

Bradman is as ruthless as a machine. He gives nothing away, and no matter how many runs he has made, he remains cool and smiling, determined not to leave the crease until the bowler earns his wicket.

## F J C GUSTARD

We feel convinced that there is no bowling in the world that would cause him even momentary uneasiness, and that if one man could 'make a team', the Ashes would be booked in advance.

## W R HAMMOND

He had a capacity I have never seen equalled in any other cricketer of docketing his cricket in one part of his mind and never letting any other event intrude there.

### BRUCE HARRIS

When there is cricket about Bradman becomes number one.

It would be a prudent bargain for any opposing captain to pension him off at 60 runs an innings and cry quits.

### MAX HARRIS

*. . . studying Bradman at close quarters one comprehends the greatness of his stature in the history of the game came from his being the fastest thinker in the business.*

### R N HARVEY

Bradman left us in no doubt that he wanted us to go through the tour unbeaten—and this we did, to establish a record unchallenged among touring teams to England.

### V S HAZARE

He was the only batsman I saw against whom all bowling looked innocuous . . .

### GEORGE HELE

England captain G O Allen always claimed bowlers win Test matches, but made one exception and that exception was Don Bradman.

### C HILL

*I wonder whether Bradman will ever get tired of making runs.*

### SIR JACK HOBBS

Our great stumbling-block is Bradman. He is too good—an absolute host in himself.

An amazing cricketer; in a class alone as a batsman and fielder.

He never gets excited when he scores a century for he can settle down for the second hundred almost as though he had just started his innings.

### GERALD HOWAT

Bradman, it seemed, had added a new dimension to the game and bowlers needed to be found to get him out.

### RAY ILLINGWORTH / KENNETH GREGORY

*A day in the sun watching Bradman at his most magnoperative, with Tyldesly and Leyland each bowling an over in 34 seconds. Superman chased by two Keystone Cops.*

### C L R JAMES

He was standing back and lashing the ball to the off-boundary in a way that lifts him head and shoulders above all other players I have ever seen.

### D R JARDINE

He almost gave the impression of having made up his mind that a rate of scoring of anything less than eight runs an over was beneath his dignity.

### I W JOHNSON

The difference between Bradman and the rest was that he might score 250 in that period, while the others would do well if they reached a century.

## C E KELLEWAY

Success in life always comes from the driving force that pushes us onward to a goal we desire to reach. With Don Bradman that driving force stays with him during the whole time he is at the crease, showing what a command his mind has over his actions . . .

Don carried the responsibility thrust upon his young shoulders like a veteran used to many campaigns.

## J M KILBURN

*Bradman could virtually guarantee a century innings every time he played in a Test match.*

## A F KIPPAX

Bradman's innings eclipsed anything we have seen in Australia before.

## J C LAKER

I can never remember Bradman letting a ball go by without playing a shot. He was streets ahead of anyone else and just couldn't be rattled.

## H LARWOOD

The bowler who is confronted by Bradman and doesn't think, doesn't bowl for long.

Then came Bradman and his presence made the difference. He was the human catalyst for whom the sharp prong of body-line was shaped.

## F G LAVERS

By sustained brilliance Bradman has established new standards of Test batting. He played and hit as he willed.

## LAURENCE LE QUESNE

Single centuries no longer seemed magnificent: double and triple centuries were the milestones of the new kind of cricket that Bradman introduced to the world.

## TONY LEWIS

Bradman had immense natural skill as well as huge concentration of mind.

## PHILIP LINDSAY

Few of my memories can equal that warm day at Lord's when, unconquerable, Don Bradman stood with the impish glee of a boy doing what he liked with the ball.

## ALAN McGILVRAY

As a batsman he had no peer.

He was at once the warrior, who would take a bowler apart with the ruthlessness that is the preserve of a few, and the artist, who would caress the ball so sweetly, with dancing feet and flowing strokes that were all grace and beauty.

## A A MAILEY

*Bradman probably sits up in the middle of the night and roars with laughter at such feeble attempts to get him out.*

Bradman never made the mistake common to many, of thinking that personal popularity is more potent than success.

### G D MARTINEAU

. . . he demolished records right and left, running up double and triple centuries against the greatest bowlers of the day, until he averaged three figures and emphasised more than ever the mastery of bat over ball.

### JIM MATHERS

*Don Bradman gave cricket statisticians enough material yesterday to work out a Chinese puzzle.*

### H F MATHEWS

I well remember, when he reached 250, the people around me expressing their amazement, and dismay, very volubly, when what must have been a Cockney retorted: 'Blimey, what are you worrying about? It's only a quarter of a thousand.'

### SIR ROBERT MENZIES

He believes in the virtue of concentrating all your mind upon the job in hand. He therefore plays to win.

### CLARENCE MOODY

Don Bradman is the miracle, confirming in the most striking fashion my contention, based on a long experience of Tests, that the country which possesses a super-champion batsman will invariably win a rubber.

## A G MOYES

Aloof? What nonsense! Or is it the old parable of the beam and the mote?

Nothing can alter the fact that Bradman's record against the bowling he has faced on all wickets has never been equalled. Indeed, it has never been approached.

He could be deaf to everything but the ticking of the clock if the game was to be saved, and he could move like a whirlwind when the time came for aggression.

. . . when a man, on all types of pitches, scores 117 centuries in 334 innings in first-class cricket, averaging 95.14 an innings, it is so stupendous that it must be accepted.

## 'NEWS CHRONICLE'

As long as Australia has Bradman she will apparently be invincible . . .

## W A OLDFIELD

*By this time Bradman's huge scores came with such regularity that they were more or less taken for granted . . .*

## W J O'REILLY

Tate finally admitted that he had no answer for the young Australian's outstanding batting gift.

## JOHN PARKER

His cricket, from first to last, was total dedication. Matches were meant to be won, and won by the largest margin possible.

### WILLIAM POLLOCK

It is never 'impossible' to bowl Hammond, but it sometimes is 'impossible' to bowl Bradman.

All the shots were his, the whole field his kingdom.

### DANIEL REESE

When batting his whole attitude was one of eagerness for runs. The bowler tried harder, the fieldsmen became keener, the public sat up and watched.

### 'REFEREE'

*The Tests would be fair if it wasn't for Don.*

### 'REUTERS'

For almost 20 years this diminutive farmer's son, invariably wearing the collar of his white cricket shirt turned up, has been making scoreboards—and turnstiles—behave like adding machines gone wild.

### W RHODES

I bowled against them all from 1900 to 1930 . . . Hobbs, W G Grace, Trumper, Ranji and many more, but Don Bradman was the greatest.

### V Y RICHARDSON

*Don Bradman is the only batsman I would have offered 100 runs every time he came in to bat against my team on the understanding that he threw his wicket away when he reached his century.*

## PHIL RIDINGS

He had such marvellous concentration, and he always wanted to make big hundreds . . .

## R C ROBERTSON-GLASGOW

*So must the ancient Romans have felt on hearing of the death of Hannibal.*
*(on Bradman's retirement)*

But numbers alone cannot express Bradman's stature nor tell how great a part of Australia's team he was.

## RAY ROBINSON

When isolated happenings, sometimes unexplained, are fitted together they make a pattern which leads to a truer valuation of his unparalleled achievements, too often taken for granted.

In his fight against the hardest antagonist he ever faced, ill-health, I found even more to admire than in any of the marvels he performed in the glow of his youth. His wonderful comeback was a triumph of the spirit.

If there was bowling to be whipped, a single to be stolen, a cheque to be written, he was the one with the lash, dash and cash to do it . . .

## IRVING ROSENWATER

Thus ended an era, the like of which cricket had never seen. It had spanned 20 years and, apart from the war, the name Bradman was the mightiest single influence of the time.

Bradman not only altered cricket but he altered cricket watching and cricket thinking . . .

## 'SECOND SLIP'

> *There are those who say that he cannot get any better, but when a genius of this nature crops up there is no telling what he may do.*

### H SHEAFFE

In Don, we have a man who has taken cricket to heart, and one who has developed control over his feelings.

### S J SOUTHERTON

Leading off with 226 in the First Test Match at Brisbane, he followed with 112 in the next at Sydney, 167 in the Third at Melbourne, and 299 not out at Adelaide in the Fourth.

*(versus South Africa 1931/32)*

### K STACKPOLE

He probably cruelled cricket for every batsman who followed him by making one mammoth score after another so easily.

### E W SWANTON

He went on and on, over after over, hour after hour, hitting the ball with the middle of the bat. There was an inevitability about his play that brought the bowler to despair.

### GRAHAM TARRANT

Bradman was the greatest run-getter of all time, dominating all bowlers to an extent that no one else has done before or since.

### M W TATE

*Pin him down? Of course not! I bowled every
ball to get the little devil out.*

### A A THOMSON

Bradman eventually became master of all of them, but his
mastery was all the greater because those with whom he
strove were in their various ways masters in their own right.

. . . they will have seen a character filled, nay, obsessed, with
an inexorable determination to do a particular thing,
unaided, better than anyone else in the world.

### 'THE TIMES'

He does not merely break records; he smashes them . . .

Bradman possesses a certain cocksure alacrity which is good
to see.

### F H TYSON

. . . the slender Australian was driven by the motivational
factor of independence: the desire to express himself in
terms of excellence in a game in which he outstripped his
fellows.

### UNKNOWN NEWSPAPER

*This Bradman is lion-hearted, physically and
figuratively. He made a double century
despite the whirlwind rib-breaking shock tactics
of Larwood.*

### R B VINCENT

. . . he has shown a sureness of scoring power to which there
seemed no limit.

### PAT WARD-THOMAS

And when Bradman is minded to do anything, no matter what, he excells at it.

### SIR PELHAM WARNER

You may talk of Alexander, Hercules, Trumper and Macartney, but this young Australian is a super-batsman and the equal of anyone.

No richer and more vivid pages in international cricket have been written than those of 1930, with Australians towering in the ascendant, piloted by sparkling little Don Bradman.

### ROY WEBBER

Australia were beaten only three times in the 92 matches in which Bradman played . . .

*(games played in England)*

### TOM WEBSTER

Another unpleasant day at the Oval. That beloved gift of nature—*rain*—came down and stopped further Bradman play . . .

### E M WELLINGS

Don Bradman is a little man who has far outstripped all the good big 'uns of his time.

. . . the most amazing scoring machine ever, a phenomenon to whom nothing in the batting line is impossible.

### P A WESTBROOK

Another reason for Don's success is his remarkable will to win—his almost unequalled power to achieve.

### R S WHITINGTON

Then, in 1930, along boomed Bradman . . .

### TREVOR WIGNALL

*If he has a fault at all, it is that he makes cricket look too much like child's play.*

Once his eye was in, however, he did everything except make his bat recite.

. . . there is absolute accuracy in the statement that when he is absent this Australian side is *Hamlet* without the Prince.

What we needed today was not six bowlers, but a battalion of them, and even at that we could have done with a machine gun when Bradman had got his eye in.

### R E S WYATT

He continued just the same after he got his first century, and even after he'd got a double century.

### N W D YARDLEY

That was Bradman's chief lesson to cricketers—never ease up.

*'Bring out your finest bowlers in their most towering form and he would perform witheringly upon them...'*

## DENZIL BATCHELOR

## 'THE ADVERTISER'

The power behind his hits, particularly vicious hooks off the fast bowlers, was obvious from the fact that although Wyatt placed the field deeper and deeper, Bradman smashed the ball past it.

## DAVID R ALLEN

He was without doubt the most relentless punisher of the bad ball—and of the marginally imperfect delivery.

## H S ALTHAM

*He is the finest hooker in the world and can direct his stroke at will anywhere from wide mid-on to fine leg with the vital, and very rare security of hardly ever lifting the ball . . .*

## JOHN ARLOTT

Then came the steamroller tactic; a century for Bradman— the repeat curtain performance which was what the crowd had come to see . . .

Give an English Test batsman—or an Australian, other than Bradman—six indifferent balls, and he will probably hit them for three fours, a couple of twos and a single. If Bradman received six indifferent balls he would hit each one of them for four.

Bradman came in, and Laker posted three short legs close to the bat. Bradman at once hit him for four to long-off, against the spin.

## E H M BAILLIE

Not for him was the passive role: he must be at the bowler's throat all the time with a grip that was never, or seldom, relaxed.

### E W BALLENTINE

On the fast-rising wicket Bradman was able to exploit his magnificent late cut fearlessly and with great power. This is one of the prettiest and most dangerous strokes in cricket. Bradman is its master.

### ERIC BARBOUR

*But perhaps the most outstanding feature of his amazing psychology is his relentlessness. He may relax physically, but never mentally, and he certainly has no mercy.*

He loves to hit and to hit hard—to place the ball just out of reach of fieldsmen—to punish the bowler who is overawing the batsman.

### RALPH BARKER

The bowling was being scientifically liquidated. Ball after ball crashed into the white fencing, by far the majority of them in an arc from cover-point to mid-off, the finest shot in cricket. No one could stop them.

### DENZIL BATCHELOR

'The Don' not only butchered the bowling, he took a cruel delight in his total mastery, as a kookaburra takes a cackling joy in breaking the necks of snakes.

Impudence! That was the word for 'the Don' when he was at his matchless best.

I remember him at his best destroying Fleetwood-Smith, foot, horse and guns, in a double century at the Sydney Cricket Ground.

The ravishing hook off Barnes was no better than elegant cutting off Allen, the slash past long-off from Voce's violent thunderbolt, or the absolute mastery with which Verity, that hope of the side, was punched, carved, clouted, cuffed, heaved and wheedled to the boundary, girdling every point of the compass.

Bradman, cheered all the way to the wicket, began with a melodramatic cavalry charge, slashing and sabring Allen for repeated boundaries.

## A V BEDSER

*He had all the strokes—and the will and nerve to crush a bowler's heart.*

## A J BELL

To bowl to him is heartbreaking. He takes risks but never seems to pay the cost which his temerity deserves.

## R BENAUD

At Lord's, Bradman's 254 was an innings that made watchers think, perhaps correctly, that they would never again see such dominating batting in this class of cricket.

'Another Bradman' is a favourite phrase of Australian critics when they believe they have discovered one to match the greatest run-getter of all time and the most merciless slaughterer of bowlers.

## W E BOWES

Hedley [Verity] and I talked about our duels with a marvellous batsman many times. I think the two of us got more pleasure, with all the stick he gave us and all the problems he set us, bowling to Don than any other batsman.

## TERRY BRINDLE

No batsman will ever again dominate bowlers and fieldsmen the way Bradman did over an entire career.

## GERALD BRODRIBB

Bradman had slaughtered the bowling, and one of the biggest cheers of the day was when Tate bowled a maiden over to him.

## F R BROWN

When he had made 100, he took a fresh guard. When he had made 200, he took guard again.

## FRANK BROWNE

*Something new and fearsome, a force of horrifying potential, had come to Test cricket.*

The runs didn't merely flow. They boiled like a maelstrom from hooks, cuts, fine, square, and late, and drives to on and off that burned the grass . . .

There was something inhuman about the savagery of his strokes.

## LINDSAY BROWNE

Bowlers sensed that Bradman's sole aim was to make them

look silly—and, at times, to make them look silly was in fact his objective.

### ALEX BUZO

In 1934 the English paid for it. The retribution of a spooked genius is a terrible thing to see.

### 'THE BYSTANDER'

Macartney, in all conscience, was an impudent striker of the ball, but he was a cautious miser compared with this young man.

### SIR NEVILLE CARDUS

*Never before this hour, or two hours until close of play, and never since, has a batsman equalled Bradman's cool deliberate murder or spifflication of all bowling.*

This was the beginning of the most murderous onslaught I have ever known in a Test match.

Bradman's fires blaze forth, threatening to consume England; there is no argument about the name of the game's greatest match-winning stroke-player when Bradman is Bradman.

The power and ease, the fluent, rapid, vehement, cold-blooded slaughter were beyond sober description.

No bowler was able to keep him quiet at his best; all were put to the sword, massacred without the turning of a hair.

Later in the day the innings became a Juggernaut, and the field a shambles.

But, as I say, he combined mass production with the performance of swift and often thrilling strokes, murderous of intent and execution.

In his heyday no known species of bowler could keep him quiet or stay his course, and despite the pace of his scoring he hardly ever lifted the ball unbeautifully.

He would not for hours even batter them—no, a contemptuous flick here, a sardonic cut there, a provoking drive on either side of the wicket.

Day after day he cut and drove and hooked bowlers right and left, never raising the ball from the ground.

He cut and hooked G O Allen that evening until it seemed that soon his bat must be red hot and catch fire.

. . . J C White the untouchable, or at least the scarcely driveable. To his first ball Bradman leaped yards out of his crease and drove it to the long-on rails, near the clock at the nursery end . . .

### CLIF CARY

. . . consider the number of occasions he faced an unknown bowler, wrested the initiative from his early deliveries, and often slashed and hit him into insensibility.

### A P F CHAPMAN

*Bradman's innings was truly magnificent; but confound him all the same.*

There is nothing to say about this match except that Bradman is a definite menace to English cricket.

### RAY COLMER

He pulled every shot out of the bag in a display of run-getting that worked up quickly to a hurricane rate. He reached his 150 in even time.

### D C S COMPTON

Bradman went on and on in that first Test and gave our attack a terrible mauling . . .

If any should doubt the crushing power of his strokes, please, I beg you, take the word of one who fielded on the boundary to him and watched a round red bullet repeatedly pass at unstoppable speed, and placed with such precision that I had no earthly chance of getting within reach.

### LORD LEARIE CONSTANTINE

*He pities none. If he can make any bowler look foolish, he will do it. If he can smash a man's averages so much that the man is dropped from big games for the season, he will spend his last ounce of energy and strain his wonderful sighting to do just that.*

### 'CRICKETER'

The advent of Bradman settled the match and, I believe, the rubber. His onslaught on the English bowling was ferocious.

### A C M CROOME

. . . play resolved itself in each case into a duel between England's bowlers and fielders on the one side and one young Australian on the other; and no one has any doubts as to who had the best of it.

## BRIAN CROWLEY

*No player before, or since, has even approached
this remarkable individual's relentless
dedication and almost supernatural talent in
the business of scoring runs.*

### 'DAILY EXPRESS'

The crowd saw a man aflame with cricket's first instinct—to
hit the ball more often, harder, and further.

### 'DAILY MAIL'

Critics of Bradman have declared that his play is
unorthodox, just as Napoleon's opponents always
complained that the great Corsican did not strictly follow
the rules of war.

### 'DAILY TELEGRAPH'

Bradman proceeded like a flashing robot. The crowd was
very silent, and could only see Bradman as a menace.

. . . who else shall fitly do honour to such a slaughter of
batsmen's records as that accomplished by a hero of the
eminence of Bradman?

## KEN DALBY

Inexorable, ruthless, insatiable, 'the Don' pressed on
through the evening session with the same computer-like
efficiency . . .

. . . and Bradman was still there to bid farewell with a
Headingley average of 192, when Harvey hit the winning
runs with 15 minutes to spare. O dig the grave and let me
die . . .

## ANTHONY DAVIS

*He made fools of the English bowlers but the English crowds, with national masochism, did not care; they adored him all the more.*

## E W DOCKER

No one ever said 'Poor Don' to him without suffering for it, if flesh and blood and sheer dogged skill and courage could make them suffer.

What did Bradman think of him? 'Put him on again after tea,' said Bradman, 'and we'll see.' Freeman's first over after tea was sensational. Bradman drove the first ball for 4, then 6, 6, 4, 6, 4. Thirty runs off a six-ball over created a new record in English cricket.

## CHRISTOPHER DOUGLAS

. . . Larwood had a nightmare vision of himself bowling over after over on those rock-hard pitches, temperatures up in the hundreds and Bradman flogging him into the parched outfield until the ball became like a bundle of old rags.

## SIDNEY DOWNER

Bradman proceeded to play an innings of great passion. He ran in to meet Larwood in his third over, and hit him past cover at a speed faster than thought.

## L B DUCKWORTH

*He was the despair of all bowlers . . .*

## W J EDRICH

Bradman gave our bowling the worst flogging in its history at Leeds in 1930, when he made 334 in his first innings . . .

He was lordly; he directed the ball round the boundaries, steering it as neatly between the exhausted fieldsmen under that glittering sky as if he were playing billiards in his shirtsleeves.

## 'EMPIRE NEWS'

Came 'the Don'—a smiling, carefree cavalier of the crease . . .

## H J ENTHOVEN

As a brilliant demonstration of scientific hitting I have never seen it remotely approached.

## T G EVANS

'The Don' did the same to four consecutive balls. It was amazing. All I could do was stand and watch, unable to prevent those fours.

## G A FAULKNER

The impression I got of Bradman yesterday was that there was no bowler playing capable of getting him out . . .

## P G H FENDER

. . . Bradman only received 448 balls in scoring his 334 runs. That is a rate equivalent to almost exactly four and a half runs per over all the time he was there. Truly magnificent.

## W H FERGUSON

*In the summer of 1930 a cricketing machine, by name of Donald Bradman, played havoc around the county grounds of England, pulverising the finest bowlers in the land, shattering records right, left and centre, and making a tour debut the like of which will surely never be seen again.*

Only one theory concerned Don Bradman—the theory that the harder he hit the ball, the farther it would travel.

Don was a phenomenon with a bat. When he was in the mood—and that was nearly all the time—he would pulverise the bowlers, indulging in what I make no apology for describing as picturesque massacre.

## J H FINGLETON

He liked nothing better than slaughtering bowlers and critics alike.

Bradman put Mailey in the stock that day for all to see. Then he hanged, drew and quartered him. Mailey was butchered to make another Bradman holiday.

Bradman at the wickets was completely at ease and at rest until the ball began its apologetic advance towards him.

That grin was the cheekiest, the most challenging, and the most confident thing I have seen in sport.

. . . every bowler, every fieldsman, every spectator in Bradman's heyday sensed that he was using not a bat so much as an axe dripping with the bowler's blood and agony.

Music to him was the crash of the ball against the fence . . . He knew no pity.

It warmed the cockles of one's cricketing heart to see once more his flashing footwork, his dazzling stroke-play, the audacity of the man, a cover drive and then, magically and murderously, his paralysing pull.

### C B FRY

Frankly, I do not know what the class of bowling has been, because Don has just gutted its quality.

Such humour in his batting! He smashes with a sort of sardonic smile in his strokes. When the runs are up he hazards a bit of a lark. He really does.

### SIR GEORGE FULLER

. . . the youth was destined to electrify England as a batsman. Don Bradman was his name . . .

### GEORGE VI, KING

*Tell me, Mr Ferguson, do you use an adding machine when 'the Don' comes in to bat?*
*(to W H Ferguson)*

### ALAN GIBSON

He suffered from Bradman, like everybody else who had to bowl at the blighter . . .

*(on J C White)*

What Bradman did to Tate in 1930 an Englishman can hardly bear to recollect.

### ALF GOVER

He would get runs off your best deliveries and murder your bad ones.

### T W GRAVENEY

There has never been anybody to touch Bradman as a director of attacks . . .

## BENNY GREEN

The thunderbolt duly arrived and again destroyed the England side.

## C V GRIMMETT

Don massacred bowling that was less than good length.

## W E HALL

He was so much the master that he destroyed that sense of contest between bat and ball which is vital to cricket.

## R A HAMMENCE

*. . . Bradman made 369 to eclipse Clem Hill's record of 365 . . . Don't mention my name, but I partnered Bradman for part of it and we made 356 in 181 minutes.*

## W R HAMMOND

His whole career demonstrates his merciless will to win.

. . . but not many of us, I think, have the ruthless capacity of a Bradman to perfect such a power as he did.

## MAX HARRIS

*Emotion had no place whatsoever in Bradman's cricket mien.*

## R N HARVEY

In his stroke-play Bradman was a law unto himself. He murdered substandard bowling effortlessly and he could do the same to any bowling in the world.

### V HAZARE

He just did what he liked with our bowling.

The opposing attack was the best in the world and was shrewdly and ruthlessly handled by Bradman.

### ALAN HILL

Don Bradman did not fumble about after courtesies with either the pen or the bat.

### C HILL

But cricket at no time has had such a consistent run-getter and match winner as Bradman. Keep on breaking records, Don! You play the game in the true cricket spirit.

### SIR JACK HOBBS

His pull against a slow ball is harder than any other batsman's I have seen for a generation.

. . . the pace with which he sends the ball to the boundary is simply amazing.

### T HOWARD

You have all heard of the wonderful efforts of these boys, particularly those of Don Bradman, who on his first visit staggered England. They were not ready for such mastery . . .

### GERALD HOWART

Old campaigners like Maurice Tate and Jack White, newcomers to Test cricket like Gubby Allen and Walter Robins, were flayed without mercy.

## MARGARET HUGHES

I couldn't turn over in my mind again any of Bradman's shots, for they were gone practically before I had time to see them.

## SIR LEN HUTTON

Bradman was always looking to attack the ball and he played shots that other batsmen would not even have attempted.

## R ILLINGWORTH/KENNETH GREGORY

*Very soon the ball ceased to be new save by a pedantic definition, for Bradman swotted it to all parts of the field.*

Whether Bradman played forward or back to Geary, and whether his bat was straight or crooked, none knew; the fielder glimpsed a blur, then trotted off like a retriever.

Himself an Everest, he awaited the assault of various bowlers and generally rewarded them with an offputting avalanche.

## JACK INGHAM

The queer potency of a Bradman innings can never be shown in figures. They're cold, chilly things.

## C L R JAMES

*A bowler bowls, Bradman makes a stroke, not a single fieldsman moves, and the ball is returned from the boundary.*

He was standing back and lashing the ball to the off-boundary in a way that lifts him head and shoulders above all other players I have ever seen.

### I W JOHNSON

Most bowlers agree that when they bowled to 'the Don' they just did not have any thoughts of getting him out.

### L H KEARNEY

Bradman's audacity was amazing, his stroke-making perfect, whilst the mighty power of his shots left the Indian fieldsmen leaden-legged and bewildered.

### J M KILBURN

His power was his delight and his use of it the greatest single attraction in the cricket of his age.

Some challenged, like Trumper; some charmed, like Ranjitsinhji; Bradman devastated—deliberately, coldly, ruthlessly.

### J C LAKER

Don Bradman was the only batsman I have known to give me an inferiority complex.

Sir Donald dedicated himself to cricket: he wanted to win in the shortest time by the biggest margin, which sounds grim—but the public got their money's worth.

### H LARWOOD

*They said I was a killer with the ball without taking into account that Bradman with the bat was the greatest killer of all.*

Bradman didn't break my heart in 1930—he just made me very, very tired.

When I bowled against Bradman, I always thought that he was out to show me up as the worst fast bowler in the world.

### F G LAVERS

Bradman dominated the play as no man has ever dominated in Test match cricket before. He is undoubtedly a cricket phenomenon.

### LAURENCE LE QUESNE

But for the fast bowler of great pace to be taken by the scruff of the neck and hit all over the field—as Larwood was by Bradman that summer—is the most violent rebuff possible.

### TONY LEWIS

And then there was that almost brutal avarice for runs—bowlers were clinically demolished.

### M LEYLAND

Bradman, tired out, bowled Leyland.

### PHILIP LINDSAY

In the second innings, the match now safe, he hit out and one marvelled at the strength of those wrists and the beauty of his drives and the swiftness of his pulls.

### G F McCLEARY

When at last he did get out I felt that the sight of his retiring back as he walked to the pavilion must have been one of the most agreeable spectacles ever witnessed by members of the fielding side.

### C L McCOOL

Bradman, of course, was way out on his own. He was the killer.

### ALAN MCGILVRAY

*Bradman was a superman among men on that tour. He was 39 when the team set off for England ... Yet he was still the best batsman in the side.*

### A MAILEY

Bradman played magnificent . . . He flogged the bowling to a standstill.

### RONALD MASON

. . . he came chirpily in to bat in the second over of the next Test at Leeds and converted the staid face of Test cricket into a kind of benevolent personal massacre, scoring 100 before lunch.

### 'MELBOURNE SUN'

A day of Bradman and a day of broken Test records . . .

### P J MOSS

Will Don Bradman ever get out except by accident in a Test match?

### A G MOYES

*He has the most scores of 300 or more in first-class cricket: 452 not out, 369, 357, 340 not out, 334, and 304. Next are Hammond and Ponsford with four each.*

He cut and drove and hooked with all the venom of his palmiest days. The ball crashed against the leg fence and flashed through the covers at a prodigious and bewildering speed.

The innings finished like a summer storm, all brilliance and ferocity, as 57 runs were struck in a mere half-hour.

Not only did he make long scores consistently—an average of one century in slightly less than each three innings—but so often he got the runs brilliantly and few others have had such ability to murder an attack.

He hit the bowlers to every quarter of the ground. He drove, hooked, and then cut with delicacy that was admirable.

### PATRICK MURPHY

Don Bradman was just too good. He destroyed the contest between bat and ball that has always been one of the chief attractions of cricket.

### 'NEWS CHRONICLE'

*It is almost time to request a legal limit on the number of runs Bradman should be permitted to make.*

### M A NOBLE

. . . he set about the bowlers and reduced their relatively high standard to a condition of impotent mediocrity.

### 'OBSERVER'

His technique and dominance made every bowler assume the role of an indispensable means to the batsman's purpose, without any other purpose.

### W A OLDFIELD

A scoring machine. Watching him batting nothing much

seemed to be happening. Then you suddenly realised that he had 70 or 80 runs on the board.

## W J O'Reilly

There was no escaping the Bradman bat when it was charged with the responsibility of smashing down all opposition.

If he decided that the object of the day was to grind a bowler flat, right down into the ground, that bowler would have had that treatment well and truly by the end of the day.

In 1930 Bradman flattened England's cricket ego. He got runs whenever they were needed and in such copious supply that he came to be recognised as the most formidable foe English bowling had ever seen.

Bradman left English cricket lying in shambles in 1930 and returned home to the plaudits of his countrymen, who treated him as though he was a gift from the gods.

The speed with which runs came from Bradman's bat left the Indian bowlers and the fieldsmen spellbound.

## John Parker

His cricket, from first to last, was total dedication. Matches were meant to be won, and won by the largest margin possible.

## L O S Poidevin

He possesses the faculty, reminiscent of the champion lawn tennis player, of never letting off anything that should be punished.

### JACK POLLARD

Bradman astonished critics of his technique by flogging the bowling to every point of the field to score 236 in 280 minutes against Worcestershire.

### WILLIAM POLLOCK

His timing was marvellous, the power he got into his strokes extraordinary. Through the covers, straight past the bowlers, round to leg, down through the slips, the ball raced from his almost magical bat.

### C H B PRIDHAM

Don Bradman, of course, has been the greatest challenge to the bowler of his generation.

### DANIEL REESE

*His slow walk to the wicket did not prepare one for the change of atmosphere that occurred the moment he took strike.*

### W RHODES

The scoring machine—that is Bradman—got to work again today and our bowlers had to pay tribute . . .

Whenever a loose ball was sent along Bradman was there to hit it safely with a wickedly vicious bat—I don't think I have seen a man so vicious with a loose ball as Bradman can be . . .

### PHIL RIDINGS

Bradman. No question. I batted with him in Shield matches and I watched him absolutely destroy the opposition. He'd hit one past a fielder's left hand and then past his right hand just for fun.

### ANTON RIPPON

English batsmen would not drive White on the half volley;
Don Bradman drove him anywhere and whenever he liked.

Bradman took the 1930 series by the scruff of the neck and
proceeded to play with such remorseless efficiency that
Australian spirits were soon soaring.

Bradman's treatment of the English bowling had been
almost inhuman. He had compiled runs with such ruthless
efficiency, such remorselessness, that all of Chapman's ruses
to remove him had failed.

### E L ROBERTS

. . . the period from January 1, 1938, to January 18, 1939,
has no parallel in cricket history. During this twelve month
period and a 'bittock' Bradman scored over 4000 runs and
averaged over 100 runs an innings.

In a minor match at Blackheath, New South Wales, in
1931/32, Bradman and Wendell Bill scored 102 in three
eight-ball overs, the former's share being 100. In these three
overs Bradman scored 10 sixes and 9 fours . . .

### R C ROBERTSON-GLASGOW

*No one ever laughed about Bradman. He was
no laughing matter.*

In Tests he altered the standard of scoring and beat all
previous ideas of arithmetic.

Then the show began. Bradman never hit in the air.
Boundaries sprang from his bat with murderous precision
and calculated profusion.

Larwood, Tate and Geary—no mean trio—were helpless. A new machine was at work. A new standard of ambition had been set.

He sliced them, into even smaller pieces; danced on them, neatly and conclusively. There'll never be another innings like his 334 against England at Leeds in 1930; never.

When I first saw Bradman, in England, he was an exquisitely heartless murderer of bowlers.

But, on 'good' pitches—that is, to the bowler, 22 yards of dumb hell—Don was, perhaps is, the nonpareil.

Attack was his method; controlled but vicious; and he kept his hitting along the ground . . .

### RAY ROBINSON

The future student of cricket history may easily be set wondering why Don ever got out—unless it was from boredom with run-making . . .

### IRVING ROSENWATER

*This mark of utter and merciless domination was born in Test cricket at Lord's in 1930, and it was Bradman who gave birth to it.*

Every time he stepped onto the field he was liable to reduce his opponents to impotence.

His temperament marked him as a man apart. In a confrontation with a bowler, there was never any doubt in Bradman's mind who was the master.

Australians were formidable opponents before Bradman, but never quite so consistently ruthless as they were after he emerged.

His hooking was venomous and his driving and cutting ruthless.

If anything, Bradman's innings was a declaration of intent, a warning and a lesson at the same time—a warning to bowlers up and down England and a lesson to those who had said his methods were too unsound for England.

He was 105 at lunch, 220 at tea, and 309 at the close— with power to add. Such indeed was the fearful domination he had imposed . . .

In prime form Bradman could annihilate any attack in the world.

### J S RYDER
Well, he just belts the hell out of every ball he can reach.

### 'SMITHS NEWSPAPERS'
Bradman has broken England's back—and the fracture never healed.

### REGGIE SPOONER
. . . it is difficult to believe that in my time anybody could have equalled his capacity as a run-getter.

### 'SPORTING LIFE'
For five and a half hours did this 21-year-old boy make mincemeat of England's bowling.

## 'SUN'

This young record-breaker in his first innings in England astonished the critics by the manner in which he flogged the bowling to every point of the ground . . .

## E W SWANTON

*What can be said without argument is that his innings, the longest in time he ever played—he batted without a chance for seven hours thirty-eight minutes—was one of the major milestones in his career.*

## GEOFFREY TEBBUTT

He is either without nerves, or his nerves are of iron; he is single-minded, calm to the point of ruthlessness, and completely confident without being cocksure.

## A A THOMSON

*The most ruthless element in his composition was his own self-discipline.*

Here was the hated enemy, the man who had battered England's bowlers to a pulp; here was the foe or iron will, the ruthless tyrant who four times had brought England to the proud foot of the conquerer. Bradman was wonderful, Bradman was terrible. He admired him, he loved him, he hated him . . .

His cricketing life was dedicated to the elementary (and elemental) proposition that every ball sent down was destined for punishment.

The holocaust of Headingley had begun.

But whenever Bradman was dismissed for a small score, somebody had to suffer for it. He treated bowlers as the late Mr Justice Avory treated criminals: with justice but without mercy.

Looking back from 1948 to 1930, when his onslaught began, he might well have been regarded as Leeds' most eminent citizen of the period, with a statue in City Square beside the Black Prince, and mounted not on a handsome charger, but on a chain-gang of English bowlers, 'couchant'.

### 'THE TIMES'

The most ardent advocate of bright cricket could ask no more of him except, perhaps, that he should occasionally— say rather oftener than once in a hundred or so—put the ball in the air.

. . . he 'pulverised' the English bowling by a display of batsmanship which, for ease of scoring, combined with absolute security, was beyond all criticism.

### W VOCE

*There's no ruddy best ball to bowl at him.*

### SIR PELHAM WARNER

No bigger than a cloud the size of a man's hand when he first appeared, he was destined to plague and dominate our bowlers for nearly a quarter of a century, and to write his name in very big letters in the chronicles of the game.

He plagued and dominated our bowlers for as long as he played.

He appeared to hypnotise the bowlers and to decree the length they should bowl to him.

Ironmonger, a most accurate left-hander, invariably kept men on the defensive, but Bradman smote him hip and thigh, and scored his century in a couple of hours or less.

### ROY WEBBER

Using almost all the strokes, he completely dominated and slaughtered the county bowling in a display that enthralled the Saturday crowd.

. . . but Bradman scored 132 in 95 minutes before lunch on the first day in a dazzling display . . .

### R S WHITINGTON

But when his team still needed runs or when he was on the brink of records, Don was not at all fussy about the bowling on which he fed.

Bradman considered attack the best and most devastating form of defence.

Don Bradman could hook the bumper like King Richard the Lionheart battle-axed Saladin and his Saracens below the walls of Jerusalem.

Bradman stands alone as the most devastating and triumphant batsman.

Larwood's first two balls were just short of a length and inches outside the off stump. The first vanished like a comet to the boundary past point, the second—an identical ball—disappeared like an impatient bullet to the square leg fence.

## TREVOR WIGNALL

*I am almost inclined to suggest, much as I like him, that he be deported to his own country, and kept there.*

### 'WISDEN CRICKETERS' ALMANACK'

At the crease he was master and the bowler, servant.

Complete master of the Essex bowlers on a fast pitch, he scored 187 in two hours five minutes, and by a wide variety of orthodox and unorthodox strokes hit 32 fours and a five.

In the second innings of his first Test match in this country at Trent Bridge he made 131, following that with 254 at Lord's, 334 at Leeds and, after failing at Manchester, putting together 232 at the Oval.

He put together many fine scores in Sheffield Shield matches and at Sydney in the first week of January eclipsed everything else by an astonishing innings of 452 not out for New South Wales against Queensland.

### W L A

Here was the lightning master of batsmanship on a great testing occasion. He swooped on the loose ones like a hawk after a small bird.

### F E WOOLLEY

He really hits the ball. Such vicious striking at the ball as his is, and always has been, rare. I have never seen fiercer.

### IAN WOOLRIDGE

*Bradman was the best. Of that there can be no doubt. He simply walked to the wicket and smashed attacks to pieces.*

### N W D YARDLEY

There was only one thing he enjoyed more than beating you by an innings and 200 runs and that was beating you by an innings and 300 runs.

Now he set his mouth hard and began to fight back, hitting the bowlers mercilessly, driving himself to the limit of his quick-footedness, his skill and his daring.

Bradman hurried on to his century, then made a typical gesture to the tired bowlers by changing his batting gloves—obviously meaning to put on another hundred.

## THE CAPTAIN
### He Had That Type of Mind . . .

*'He had that type of mind—
cool logic was his great secret.'*

SIR LEN HUTTON

## H S ALTHAM

I do not think I have ever admired anything on the cricket field so much as his leadership through those heartbreaking days at the Oval in August: his own fielding was an inspiration in itself, and as hour succeeded hour with nothing going right and the prospect of the rubber receding over a hopeless horizon, it was, one felt, his courage and gaiety that alone sustained his side.

## JOHN ARLOTT

He nursed his bowlers wisely and received magnificent service from his fielders.

When Bradman suggests an alteration to the laws of cricket he is listened to with the greatest respect.

## ALEX BANNISTER

Sir Donald was pre-eminent as a player and he carries his genius to the press box.

Clearly, the batsman who upset all values with his record scoring; the captain with the strategic reputation second to none—in short, the world's greatest cricketer . . .

## ERIC BARBOUR

I have never known a keener or shrewder student of the game. Every batsman and every bowler he has seen has been read, marked, and inwardly digested.

## S G BARNES

'The Don', a legend in his own lifetime, was knighted for his unique contribution to cricket and the 1948 Test series was the final, striking testimony to his ruthless efficiency.

. . . his brilliant pre-tour planning which would have done credit to a military strategist.

. . . but 'the Don', as I saw it, *was* the game of cricket in Australia.

### DENZIL BATCHELOR

Bradman, with Pluvius [J], out-generalled Allen with the rest of the England XI. That was the stark result of the exercise . . .

As a captain he proved sound always and, when necessary, astute.

And I remember, above all, his captaincy against 'Gubby' Allen. Two down and three to play, he saved the rubber as by divine right of kingship.

The third Test match at Melbourne was won almost in the style of a game of chess-by-correspondence: by sheer tactical superiority—bat and ball didn't come into it.

### R BENAUD

Sir Donald was easily the best selector I came across in the game anywhere in the world, not just in Australia.

I'd have given a lot to play in a side under Bradman and to be able to watch the master at work, whether with bat or in the field of captaincy . . .

### BEN BENNISON

I found him more than a profound student of cricket—he was the conquerer of cricket. He set out and meant to be king. He succeeded.

## CHARLES BRAY

| *Brilliant, I shall never forget his captaincy.* |

. . . and while I shall always remember 'the Don' for his many great innings I shall never forget his captaincy.

Yet I must confess that only on the rarest occasions have I been able to think, let alone write, that Bradman made a mistake in the handling of his bowlers or the setting of the field.

## AUSTEN BROWN

No man has done more for cricket. Don has always placed the game before financial reward.

## F R BROWN

I rate him the best captain of my time.

Bradman's record as captain speaks for itself. There was no doubt about it: he studied the job from every conceivable angle and played the game the hard way without relenting.

## FRANK BROWNE

His speech was quiet, his words few, and confined to the matter at hand.

But Bradman's last tour as Australian captain had all the grim purposefulness of Scipio's last campaign against Carthage.

There was his genius as captain, which enabled him to get the absolute best, and it was a superlative best, from his team.

## TIM CALDWELL

. . . incisive in thought, who does his homework thoroughly—more so than others—and is an outstanding administrator because of his aggressive attitude in those matters in which he believes.

## SIR NEVILLE CARDUS

*And he was a shrewd far-seeing captain who commanded from everybody an emotion less common in ordinary human nature than affection: he commanded respect.*

Bradman's fielding and his eager and sensible captaincy throughout a fearful ordeal were beyond praise; he nursed his bowlers, talked to them, put his arm in theirs between overs, and cheered them up; he was not only the team's captain but the father-confessor and philosopher.

He is the brain and vertebrae of Australian cricket, Government and executive . . . Bradman bestrides them all; he bestrides the whole history of the game . . .

Nobody has excelled Bradman's 'cricket sense', his intuitions and understanding. He must be counted among Australia's cleverest, most closely calculating cricket captains.

No cricketer had a quicker, shrewder brain than Bradman.

He respected an opponent and refused to patronise him.

## DUDLEY CAREW

*The team seem to take their cue from him as an orchestra takes it from an inspired and trusted conductor.*

## I M CHAPPELL

'You used to be a good hooker. What's happened to that shot?' That comment from Australia's greatest batsman ever convinced me it was time I re-introduced the hook shot to my range.

## LORD COBHAM

. . . an immensely powerful Australian batting side, over which the youthful phenomenon, Don Bradman, rules supreme and apparently invulnerable.

## D C S COMPTON

Bradman knew our weaknesses and went for them with the greatest skill.

You were also conscious of that thoughtful, active, penetrating brain which constantly applied itself to the individual problem of getting the particular player out.

He was the best captain that I ever played against.

In fact, judging by his careful planning, he might well have made his mark in the military sphere had he turned his thoughts in this direction!

I could have stayed up all night listening to 'the Don' talk cricket . . .

'The Don's' summing-up of the opposition is truly amazing . . .

## LORD LEARIE CONSTANTINE

Bradman was a fine skipper, and brought the art of Test captaincy to a new high level.

## TED CORBETT/JOANNE KING

Don Bradman lost his first two Tests as captain, became the only captain to win a series after being two down and was undefeated in 21 of his last 22 Tests. It is a record that is almost as incredible as his batting feats . . .

## GERRY COTTER

He was a very astute man who gave much thought to his tactics, knew how to motivate his men and, more than anyone else, could lead by example.

. . . as he settled into the job, his field-setting became very sophisticated and his captaincy grew to match his stature as a batsman.

## 'DAILY EXPRESS'

In England last summer he comported himself, both on and off the field, with outstanding dignity.

His remarkable run of Test team captaincies, his phenomenal scoring, his leprechaun fielding, his tactical sense—all these point him as the cricketer of our time.

## 'DAILY HERALD'

*At hotels he is making a point of personally thanking the staff for their attention to his team.*

## ANTHONY DAVIS

And, like a general, he looked beyond the results of individual battles to the final outcome.

As captain and Australian selector, working on and off the

field, he did much to create, build and train by 1948 one of the greatest teams ever seen.

### J C DAVIS

And Bradman is unsurpassed by any man in this or any part as a team member.

### E W DOCKER

Bradman was different because from a very youthful age he was able to give total concentration to what he was doing on the field as much as off it.

### SIDNEY DOWNER

He could well be described as the intellectual opportunist.

Don Bradman's mastery of cricket law is of the same stature as his mastery of its technique. He even sat for an umpire's examination, and passed at the top of the honours list.

### KEITH DUNSTAN

*He thought out his moves like a Russian playing chess.*

### W J EDRICH

Australia under his captaincy had shown more ruthlessness, more cold-blooded determination to win . . .

. . . and perhaps there is no one left in the game today with his extraordinary knowledge of strategy, and his gifted ability to seize a winning moment.

I rate him as the best captain of a cricket team since 1914—and perhaps ever.

### G D Evans

He was at his greatest as a captain on that tour . . . His control in the field and his field-placing were superb.

No credit is too high for 'the Don', for he revealed himself as still the great cricketer we had known in the past. He was a brilliant captain . . .

### H V Evatt

. . . he has vindicated the opinions of many that he would be a great success as captain.

### W H Ferguson

*Sir Donald Bradman is, perhaps, admitted to have been the most successful cricket captain of all time . . .*

### J R Fingleton

As a skipper he was merciless, determined from the outset in 1948 to get a record which meant as much as any to him— that of leading an unbeaten team in England.

Bradman never allowed himself to relax or relent until the objective had been achieved.

### Andy Flanagan

Bradman, as captain, is a relentless leader and gives no quarter. He never patronises his opponents . . .

### C B Fry

Bradman is an extremely intelligent, observant, and quick-witted captain.

## NORMAN GILLER

He was a shrewd, competitive and—when necessary—merciless captain who led by example.

He commanded respect at all times, and his players responded to his totally committed approach to cricket by always giving 100 per cent themselves.

Don Bradman brought to his captaincy all the powers of concentration, the efficiency and command that made him the greatest compiler of runs the game of cricket has ever known.

## A E R GILLIGAN

*Future generations will regard him not only as a very great batsman, but also as a brilliant captain and, above all, as one of the truest gentlemen who has ever worn flannels.*

## MAURICE GOLESWORTHY

This cricketing genius played in 52 Tests, 24 of them as captain, and he never lost a rubber in the five series of Tests in which he led his side.

## W E HALL

In due course we shall come to see Bradman as an inevitable part of the evolution of the game.

## W R HAMMOND

Bradman, quite rightly because of his massive performances, can speak with great weight in cricket circles today.

Undoubtedly the two greatest captains, in the art of field

setting, have both come from Australia. M A Noble in the first decade of this century, and Don Bradman in the fifth . . .

Don was one of the keenest observers of opponents who ever captained a cricket team.

. . . and Bradman is the finest modern exponent of the defensive field collaboration with fast bowling.

### JOE HARDSTAFF

*On the field he was a scrupulously fair, but ruthless opponent. He made cricket his business and his life.*

### R N HARVEY

Bradman was a great leader. His knowledge of the game is unrivalled and he directed his side on the field with great strategy and understanding.

### R J HAYTER

For Bradman the tour provided the most fitting climax possible to an illustrious career. Apart from leading Australia to continued Test dominance, he made more hundreds than any batsman in the country . . .

Bradman demonstrated his knowledge of the game in captaincy and generalship.

### V S HAZARE

He was captaining a team which later on was to be acknowledged as one of the greatest ever.

### DAVID HIGHAM

*This man is a captain.*

### C HILL

Keen and enthusiastic in everything he does, Bradman carries his men with him.

### GERALD HOWAT

Bradman 'came good' at the right time and he would be a tactician superior to all of the England captains he would later meet.

His opposite number was Bradman who, in the view of several of Hammond's colleagues, out-manoeuvred him as a tactician.

### R ILLINGWORTH

Tactically he was very good; he made precious few mistakes and he read opposing batsmen like an open book. He was sharp and tough.

### R ILLINGWORTH/K GREGORY

*... 1948 saw Bradman's Grand Army embark on a long campaign ... by September the major battles had been won and England lay prostrate under Bradman's heel.*

### I W JOHNSON

It was impossible not to be impressed or to learn by Bradman's method of captaincy.

Bradman set a field for each individual batsman. That

technique has been followed by present-day captains and has played no small part in controlling the general rate of scoring.

... he sat and talked with me for three-quarters of an hour because he didn't want me to be alone on the morning of my first Test. It was, I think, the most human thing I have encountered in sport.

### C E KELLEWAY

Don carried the responsibility thrust upon his young shoulders like a veteran used to many campaigns.

### R R LINDWALL

Under Bradman's gifted leadership, we were a powerful all-round young side.

No one could have treated me better than Bradman and, after playing under him in nearly 20 Test matches, I still say the same about him.

His deeds and consistency were nothing short of amazing, but of equal value was the feeling of supreme confidence his presence gave to the rest of the XI.

### 'LONDON STAR'

Bradman is not only the world's greatest batsman. As the years have added to his skill, he has become the perfect cricket ambassador.

### C G MACARTNEY

D G Bradman as the leader and the batsman is a host in himself.

## G F McCleary

As captain he radiates energy; his watchfulness and judgement are unfailing, and he possesses the rare and invaluable gift of keeping up the tails of his men in a tight place.

## Alan McGilvray

*Tactically and technically, Bradman was a superb captain. He could sum up the weaknesses and the strengths of players in an instant.*

Making critiques of Bradman's on-field captaincy was a very dangerous business.

He contributed long and mightily as an administrator, and his counsel is still widely sought.

He could anticipate how opponents would think. So often would he astound me by pointing out things which would completely escape my notice.

The team Bradman led to England in 1948 was quite simply the finest cricket team the world has ever seen.

As a captain he achieved exactly what he set out to achieve.

## A A Mailey

*Don Bradman's knowledge of bowlers' tactics and wicket conditions is astounding.*

His intuition, tenacity, and calculative mind have given him an individualism which demands attention . . .

That he can express a more sensible opinion than most
cricketers on any set of subjects, there is no doubt . . .

Unlike many people who attain power, Bradman has never,
to my knowledge, resorted to political intrigue or
compromise.

### CHRISTOPHER MARTIN-JENKINS

> *As captain of Australia, starting in 1936/37, he
> was as efficient and merciless as he was a
> batsman, and diplomatically he never put a foot
> wrong.*

### RONALD MASON

Without him, Australia were a fine side that could perhaps
by exercise of traditional skills be contained and possibly
mastered; with him, no such matter.

### JIM MATHERS

. . . as a team-mate with post-war players, he was freely
spoken of as guide, philosopher and friend.

### SIR ROBERT MENZIES

Bradman believed in the virtue of concentrating all his mind
on the job in hand.

For 20 years I have been Bradman's beneficiary, for he is
the greatest batsman, the most devastating stroke-maker and
most concentrating tactician I ever hope to see.

As a highly interested onlooker I was constantly fascinated
by the skill with which you controlled the game at all stages.
There are very many of us who think that we have never
seen a better or more subtle exhibition of captaincy.

## P J MILLARD

In addition to ranking still as the world's greatest batsman, he stands high among the great captains of Test cricket.

## K R MILLER

*Don has always played to win, whether batting or captaining his team in a Test match, playing a round of golf with friends, playing a game of snooker or billiards with guests on his own billiard table.*

Don has always set his men a perfect example so far as his demeanour on and off the field is concerned.

The most impressive thing about his captaincy was the ease with which he handled his men on the field.

His captaincy, his attacking nature on the field left little to be desired.

For me, what is outstanding as well about Bradman is that he is the first man who made a science out of cricket captaincy.

## A G MOYES

Bradman brought to bear on the problems of captaincy a shrewd knowledge of cricket and a keen analytical brain.

It was the end of one of cricket's most glorious eras. It marked the passing of the greatest force Test cricket has known . . . and of one of cricket's greatest captains.

. . . but his record of achievement, his rare quality of

leadership on the field or in the committee room, not forgetting his ability as a fieldsman, will ensure that his name will never die.

In later years his leadership gained in trust, and he thought faster than the other chap.

After the war there was no doubt as to who was the finest captain, offensive or defensive, in the game.

A masterly batsman, an exceptional fieldsman, a brilliant captain, he created a legend of invincibility.

He led his side with a mixture of calm, shrewd, calculated planning and intuition.

Bradman did a magnificent job for cricket on the field, in the committee room, and through advice he gave orally and in articles.

It would be presumptuous on the part of any cricketer in the world to try to tell Don anything about cricket today.

Down the years, Bradman so often has had to win, or save, a match that it has become second nature.

### 'NEWS CHRONICLE'

He has shown himself to be a captain of unsurpassed skill. He has imbued the Australian team with his own single-minded determination to win. This amazing power of concentration was the determining factor.

### 'NOTTINGHAM GUARDIAN'

My own memories of 'the Don' are of a captain . . . of a 'god' shaking hands with one of his worshippers—a nine-year-old boy, trembling with excitement—and chatting encouragingly to him.

### W J O'REILLY

*His keen analytical brain has concentrated on his plans of campaign long before the first shot was fired.*

### IAN PEEBLES

As importantly his presence lent immense morale to the team, and his captaincy was unexcelled in its judgement, discipline, and ever alert knowledge.

But no one in England has foreseen the strength of the Australian resurgence, led by the phenomenon of Don Bradman.

### JACK POLLARD

. . . Bradman's side was the best disciplined and unified of all Australian touring outfits . . .

### C H B PRIDHAM

As to captaincy—the value of which we are inclined to underestimate—have we ever seen a better Australian leader than Bradman himself?

### PHIL RIDINGS

Bradman, without doubt the finest captain Australia ever had …

## R C ROBERTSON-GLASGOW

> *Bradman is an incurable original, a gamin who gleefully longed to join the pirates, and became captain of them all.*

But, all in all, Bradman was the supreme tactician.

Most important of all, he steered Australia through some troubled waters and never grounded on the rocks.

On the field he was superb. He had seen and weighed it all. Shrewd and tough, he was not likely to waste anything in dreams of mercy.

No one ever saw Bradman not attending.

It was a coolly considered policy. Cricket was not to be his hobby, his off-hours delight. It was to be his life and his living.

## RAY ROBINSON

He developed into a speaker who won praise for his responses on behalf of his team.

To the task of captaining Australia he brought an acute cricket brain, a highly developed faculty for espying and weighing to the last pennyweight every factor bearing on success for his batting.

Outstanding in Bradman's captaincy was his field-placing. He made an exact science of setting run-tight fields to starve the batsman out.

### IRVING ROSENWATER

*Don Bradman became captain of Australia in 1936/37, and from that time Australia never lost a series against England while he was captain.*

He was now recognised by authority to possess cricketing wits as quick as his bat.

He was now a Test match captain to be feared as much as he was overwhelmingly a Test match batsman to be feared.

Having been through the fire of Test captaincy in 1936/37, Bradman matured quickly as a strategist who was never to lose a Test series in his life.

### JACK SCOTT

*In my knowledge, Bradman and Jardine stand out as the most learned on rules. Bradman can hardly be faulted. In fact, he knows more than some umpires about the game.*

### R B SIMPSON

If you were trying to improve your batting and Bradman offered to help, you would be a fool to turn him down.

### 'SPORTING GLOBE'

With his wonderful cricket brain he has imparted a tremendous amount of confidence to the players . . . His personality is such that the younger players, in which he has taken an unusually keen interest, regard him as a great leader.

Above all his personal triumphs Bradman has done this one greater thing for cricket: he has taken the bits and pieces of our prospective Test team and has blended them into the greatest cricket force in the world today.

### 'THE SPORTING RECORD'

And you can take it that all his players almost worship the turf he treads on.

### J B STOLLMEYER

*If there is anyone living who is more knowledgeable on the game of cricket than this cricketing knight then I would like to know him.*

'The Don' brought his great knowledge and perception into cricket administration after he ceased to play the game actively, and in this area his concentration was in no way less great.

### E W SWANTON

For millions have enjoyed seeing his supreme artistry in the flesh, while the game in general has been the richer for the stimulus he gave it during his playing life, and also for his wise guidance of it since his retirement 40 years ago.

It is true that we had all the bad luck going, but the fact is that 'the Don' could give poor old Wally [Hammond] a stroke a hole at captaincy and the whole thing gradually fell to pieces.

That Bradman, in his arduous role as world's best batsman and untried captain, held the key to the series comes through in all that was written about him.

In his comprehensive survey of the game, Bradman, widely regarded as the greatest batsman of all time, spoke with the authority of an elder statesman in the world of cricket.

## D TALLON

In 1946/47, under Bradman, we played the game hard and were clearly superior.

## A A THOMSON

C B Fry, who knew more about cricket as a science than any man who ever lived, except perhaps Sir Donald Bradman . . .

Nowhere was Bradman's ascendency shown more clearly than in his captaincy.

. . . he was an outstanding captain because he was pre-eminent in strength of character, in strategic knowledge of the whole game, in ceaseless thought on relevant problems and, most important, in his ability to seize the initiative and his refusal to surrender.

The same iron will which dictated the almost unbreakable concentration on his batting without cramping his scoring speed sprang from the same intelligence capable of seeing in advance all the possibilities of the game.

As a captain he had the mind of a chess-player, operated with the speed of an Olympic fencer.

In every person of quality there is a strain of the romantic and a strain of the realist; a touch of the artist and a touch of the businessman, or possibly the scientist. In Bradman the two, or rather the three strains were perfectly balanced and blended as never before or since.

### BEN TRAVERS

*In conversation with anyone so decisive and sharp-witted it is often a pleasure to be hit for four.*

### R B VINCENT

And I feel that all through his illustrious cricket career he has always been thinking, concentrating on what has to be done. Master of himself, just as he had unquestionably been master of the bowlers.

### B J WAKLEY

One of Australia's greatest and most successful captains . . .

### SIR PELHAM WARNER

He knows everything there is to be known about cricket both from the tactical and strategical viewpoint, and his judgement of a cricketer is unfailing.

### C WASHBROOK

. . . I found good cause to appreciate his field-placing and the way in which he summed up a batsman's abilities.

### ROY WEBBER

Bradman, unlike some Australian captains of the past, ensured that each member of the side received a fair share of match play . . .

### CRAWFORD WHITE

*He is still the greatest batsman in the world, and goodwill tour or not, he remains the coolest and most ruthless strategist in cricket.*

### R W WHITINGTON

Naturally, in the beginning Bradman's leadership was fallible. By the time he retired it was the object of almost universal admiration. Rarely can such profound knowledge of the game, its history and its laws have been applied so shrewdly and so implacably.

There has been no finer cricket strategist, no more profound student of the game.

### W L A

There, beyond all question, was a captain of men.

### W M WOODFULL

Bradman impressed me in a very marked degee with his genius for captaincy and field-placing.

### N W D YARDLEY

Bradman was fortunate in having such a fine side, but there can be no doubt he led it shrewdly and well.

### E C YEOMANS

Don Bradman is greater than a cricketer. No better diplomat has ever served Australia.

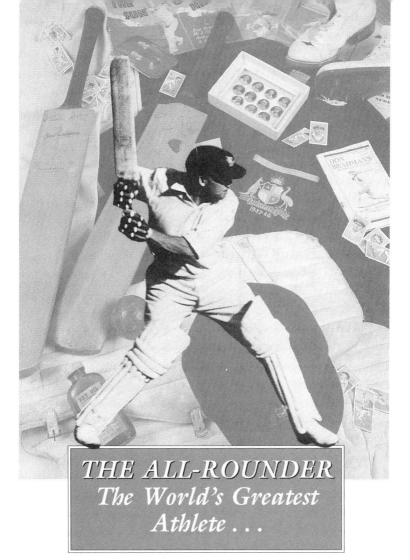

## THE ALL-ROUNDER
### The World's Greatest Athlete . . .

*'I have no hesitation in calling him the world's greatest athlete, and I am nearly tempted to throw everything overboard and write him down as the most remarkable the world has ever known.'*

TREVOR WIGNALL

## H S ALTHAM

For here is obviously a perfectly co-ordinated body,
balanced on feet as neat, and at the same time as strong, as
any professional dancer's, which ensure maximum speed and
accuracy of movement.

One cannot be bored with a man who is so tremendously
alive every moment he is on the ground . . .

. . . for he does not tire, he does not relax, and even on the
days when he is, for him, palpably out of form, a long score
remains more probable than a short one.

## JOHN ARLOTT

He stood at the crease perfectly immobile until the ball was
on its way to him, then his steps flowed like quicksilver out
of trouble or into position to attack.

He thought nothing of moving two or three yards down the
wicket to a bowler, yet, search the records, see how often
Bradman was stumped . . .

He was always a grand catcher and, when young, the fastest
and keenest of outfields.

If I were faced with a task, on a materialistic plane, I would
sooner have Bradman to work with me than any other man
I have ever met . . .

## T E BAILEY

He was so very quick on his feet that he was probably the
most difficult batsman to contain there has been.

## DENZIL BATCHELOR

The arms seemed to stretch to any length required of them. The feet did any job, however impossibly fast ...

The footwork was audacious, the wrists well sprung, the eyes saw the opportunity—if not the ball—larger and quicker than any other player of our day.

The flying Bradman took the ball inches from the fence in his fingertips and, apparently straightening while still airborne, without putting foot to ground, broke the far wicket with his throw-in.

## A V BEDSER

*Co-ordination of movement and his razor-sharp brain reached perfection.*

Whatever challenge in sport, business, writing or cricket administration, 'the Don' excelled . . .

## A J BELL

*If throwing square to the wicket he hits it from the boundary once in three times.*

His running is phenomenal.

## 'BRITISH WEEKLY'

The agile movement of Bradman's feet was worthy of a Pavlova.

## GERALD BRODRIBB

. . . but Bradman at mid-off made a brilliant stop and throw, and ran Tate out.

## F R BROWN

I have never seen a better cover point than Bradman.

In his prime his fielding in any company was quite outstanding.

## SIR NEVILLE CARDUS

It is forgotten as we wonder for ever at the runs he amassed that when he was young he had no superior as an outfielder, none more thrilling in chase and pick-up and deadly return.

His catching was equally agile; I have seen him run after a ghost of a chance on the off-side and hold a spinning miss-hit while his body was swivelling round like a top released from a whip.

Bradman, by the very quickness of his eye and feet, was born to conquer any turning ball . . .

In all his career Bradman did little that was more wonderful and so highly charged with his own force of character than his dazzling improvisations, his neck or nothing brilliance, in the face of the ruthless challenge of Jardine thrown down in 1932/33.

He ran to the pavilion, not out 309—and there was not a trace in his face of weariness; his hair was beautifully parted; he looked as though fresh from a bandbox.

## CLIF CARY

*I am positive that in whatever sphere of life he had chosen he would have been an outstanding figure.*

Search the world and it would be impossible to find a cleaner-living chap.

## D C S COMPTON

He had a marvellous gift of getting into position quicker than any batsman I have ever seen, played the ball very late, and was never off balance, or stretching out of control.

## CLAUDE CORBETT

The 'laughing cavalier' of cricket. They may nearly get his wicket; they may almost run him out; he may crack the bowling in all directions. It is just the same to Bradman. Laughter is the companion forever with him.

To know Bradman is to know as clean a type of young manhood imaginable. Full of the effervescent fun natural to a trained athlete in the full flower of a brilliant career, Bradman enjoys every moment of his cricketing life.

## M C COWDREY

*... there to slave for hour upon hour at his woods and irons. His handicap duly plunged to scratch and by the expiry of his self-imposed timetable Don Bradman was one of the finest amateur golfers in Australia. If only he had been 15 years younger Gary Player and Peter Thomson would have felt the lash of his tail.*

## A C M CROOME

Bradman stopped everything within reach accurately and easily.

He chassied out to the pitch of the good-length balls, and

altered the direction of them as well as their length to suit his purpose, so that he could drive them where the fieldsmen were not.

### 'DAILY NEWS'

He went golfing today . . . The opinion is expressed that if he practised he would probably become Australia's amateur champion.

### ANTHONY DAVIS

*He was one of the fastest fielders ever seen capable of chasing a ball, plucking it from the air and returning it to the wicket with unbelievable speed.*

He was, in fact, a splendid speaker. The roars of applause that greeted him at the end of a speech were genuine tribute . . .

### E W DOCKER

The athleticism of this performance, the number of hard-run twos and threes obtained between morning and early evening was almost beyond computation.

### CHRISTOPHER DOUGLAS

Bradman was so quick on his feet that he could have remained at the crease all day simply dodging the bouncers . . .

### SIDNEY DOWNER

Bradman's hands and wrists are small, his fingers long and narrow—a pianist's fingers.

It is that quality which makes us say of him, as Dr Johnson said of the dancing dog: 'It is not that he can do it so well that it is a source of wonderment, it is that he can do it at all.'

He dived like a swallow as the ball came near him at cover. His returns to the wicket defied vision to follow.

### H V EVATT

*Characteristic of Bradman's in-cricket is his perfect running between wickets and his shepherding of younger players during critical periods of an innings.*

Bradman's figures are necessarily silent as to important aspects of his batting. At times the speed of his scoring has been phenomenal.

### P G H FENDER

That he was the best fielder on the boundary on either side admits of no doubt . . .

### W H FERGUSON

Fielding in the deep, Don's returns were amazingly accurate and swift.

### J H FINGLETON

Therein lay much of his greatness—a quicker brain, a quicker judgement than any other batsman I have seen.

Bradman was richly endowed in all that went toward making the champion, and in none more so than in his twinkling, magical feet.

His feet took him into immediate position to offset swerve, swing or break bowling; his running feet took him three and even four yards up the pitch . . .

His lithe, compact body was a powerhouse of latent electricity until the switch of a ball released was turned, and then his brightness flashed in all directions.

Bradman has such a strong, straight throw that nobody could be tempted to run.

Bradman preferred to listen to music rather than submit himself to the gaze of his admirers by going down to dinner.

## C B FRY

He moves on his feet ever so neatly and ever so easily in good time. He is poised on the ball of the feet not the flat. Like a good dancer. More, he does trust his eye utterly. Not afraid really to wait and see.

Bradman has a gem of a body for batsmanship, conformation perfect: hence perfect poise. A bundle, beautifully shaped, of what the Greeks called harmony.

He has always been one of the best after-lunch or after-dinner speakers—doing what comes naturally. He is witty.

## T W GRAVENEY

His footwork was quick, his balance exact, his timing perfect and his shots—particularly on the on-side—powerful and deadly accurate.

## F J C GUSTARD

As a deep fieldsman he is brilliant, his work in front of the pavilion at the Oval Test in 1930 being particularly scintillating.

## W R HAMMOND

By the most astounding cat-like leap, and simultaneous pick-up and return, he threw my wicket down while I was still a yard out of my crease.

## E GORDON HARBURG

. . . what struck me about Bradman's batting was his cat-like actions, and how hard he hits the ball for a little fellow.

## JOE HARDSTAFF

*My feet feel tired when I think of him.*

There was no limit to the endurance and skill of this slight, lean Australian.

## MAX HARRIS

If the career of the administrative Bradman was to be assessed, it would probably be revealed as the most positively creative element in his quiet life, apart from his batting years.

As a public speaker he is a natural droll. Again it is that latent brain-speed which enables him to ad lib, to produce the sharp relevant commonsensical quip.

## GEORGE HELE

*He was standing at square leg with the ball in his hand. With three successive throws he hit the one stump visible to him three times . . .*

### E H HENDREN

And of course—we always get back to this, don't we—a fine fielder.

### C HILL

His footwork and wrist action are perfect. He has a wonderful eye, endurance and stamina.

### SIR JACK HOBBS

Had I known of his reputation in the field I would not have responded to Phil's call for a third run. The ball came whizzing in to the wicket-keeper like a gun-shot. I was easily out.

### W M HUGHES

His footwork was wonderful, his timing superb, he was master of every stroke.

### SIR LEN HUTTON

He was also a superb fielder, as good as any in his prime, with speed, pick up and deadly return.

Hedley [Verity] said Bradman was so difficult to bowl against because he was so quick on his feet.

### JACK INGHAM

*Bradman is not a showman, though every move he makes on the field screamingly advertises his presence. There is so much he does that no one else can do.*

### C L R JAMES

The ball seemed so easy to hit. It wasn't. The quick

judgement and rapid footwork had made everything else
into child's play.

### L H KEARNEY

His footwork and fast running between wickets for a
batsman who is on the borderline of being termed a veteran
were amazing.

### J C LAKER

But I do think that he was ready to move, that he was on
his toes, earlier than most. And that his batting instinct
allowed him to move into position for a stroke earlier than
almost any player the game has known.

### H LARWOOD

> *There was only one man we were after—*
> *Bradman. There'll never be another like him.*
> *I've never seen such quick footwork.*

Bowling to Australia's batsmen was rather like potting
pheasants on the wing, but with Bradman it was like trying
to trap a wild duck, his movements were so swift.

He did all the things you didn't want him to do. He had
the quickest eye of any batsman I ever met.

### F G LAVERS

Bradman today differed from these masters because virility is
inherent in his art. He was superb, indeed dazzling, all the
time.

He has the feet of a dancing master: they take him to
positions inaccessible to the average batsman, and his
wonderful eye and wrists do the rest.

### TONY LEWIS

*As a teenager, Don Bradman had been a
sprinter, a champion runner, never beaten.*

### PHILIP LINDSAY

The moment the ball has been bowled, Bradman, one feels,
has made up his mind what he will do with it . . .

Few of my memories can equal that warm day at Lord's
when, unconquerable, Don Bradman stood with the impish
glee of a boy doing what he liked with the ball.

### G F McCLEARY

Nor is it only as a batsman that he is great. In the field he is
among the best: untiring, fleet of foot, swift in his pounce
upon the ball, and deadly with the throw in.

His muscles are beautifully co-ordinated and instantly
responsive to the dictates of his brain. It is a pleasure to
watch the movements of that strong and supple body.

### A A MAILEY

*Don Bradman will be remembered as one of the
most remarkable sportsmen who ever graced
the sporting stage of any country. Bradman
is an enigma, a paradox; an idol of millions
of people . . .*

### 'A MAN IN THE CROWD'

Bradman, with two economical dancing steps, made it a
half-volley and played it straight to the screen. That single
stroke was a revelation.

### CHRISTOPHER MARTIN-JENKINS

But he was as honest and level-headed in his business activities as he was in his approach to cricket, and almost equally successful.

### G D MARTINEAU

His full-speed picking up and throwing-in from the Oval boundary, saving the second run, were movements of sheer beauty.

### RONALD MASON

He had all the strokes, was lightning of foot and eye, had an ice-cool temperament and boundless stamina; was, to crown all, ruthless, ambitious, successful.

### JIM MATHERS

*Apart altogether from the runs Bradman scores, his effort was a physical feat of endurance that should provide inspiration for the imagination of some of the specialty writers of health advertisements . . .*

### SIR ROBERT MENZIES

In him we have witnessed the supreme cricketing combination: the quick eye, the instantaneous muscular response, the incisive and flashing intelligence.

I have been on the same bill with him for after-dinner speeches, and have marvelled at him. He has the born after-dinner speaker's faculties of wit, flexibility, and quick feeling for atmosphere.

### P J MILLARD (1947)

Of the 72 players who took part in the Sheffield Shield games in 1927/28 season, only one remains in big cricket—Don Bradman.

### A G MOYES

Don d'Artagnan of the Willow. The young man with a flashing blade, full of the spirit of adventure.

Later he moved to the covers and was again a champion, his speed, his certainty in gathering the ball, his fast accurate throw, giving life and zest to the game.

Don's knowledge is not confined to cricket. He has a profound knowledge of many things.

He has the mental, moral, and physical make-up that tends to greatness.

### NEWSPAPER REPORT OF 1939

*Australia's cricket captain, D G Bradman, last night defeated the former Davis Cup tennis player, D P Turnbull, by three games to two in the final of the amateur squash racquets championship of South Australia at the Amateur Sports Club.*

### 'NOT OUT'

Bradman's batting had all the verve and joyousness of a boy in his teens . . .

Bradman has the elasticity and the fibre of a first-class athlete . . .

He is, I think, the fastest man to the ball I have ever seen.

Some of the Bradman returns from the outfield, ever on the full to the far wicket, were as fine as the finest one ever saw . . .

### W A OLDFIELD

Watch Bradman field a ball! Here is no waste of energy, but should the occasion demand the ball comes true as a bullet direct to the wicket-keeper, invariably bail high.

### MICHAEL PAGE

. . . an athlete of international stature, whose genius belonged to the whole of mankind rather than to one nation alone.

### E J PALMER

*I also seem to remember that, young as he was, he drove a car superbly and could, perhaps, have been a world champion racing driver.*

### MICHAEL PARKINSON

For a kid in a pit village to be breast-fed on the Bradman legend, 12 000 miles away from where it started, is a clear indication of Bradman's unique position, not just in cricket, but in all sport.

### IAN PEEBLES

Bradman was fast, decisive and an unfailing judge of speed and distance.

Apart from his supreme ability as a batsman, his astonishing physical and mental stamina meant that he could sustain a high rate of scoring over long periods, resulting in enormous scores achieved at record speed.

There was a galvanic quality about the speed and decision of this move beyond any batsman I have ever previously seen.

### JACK POLLARD

He was generally rated as the best fieldsman in the Australian side, shading even the tremendously athletic Vic Richardson . . .

### W H PONSFORD

*The reason is very simple. Don sees the ball about two yards sooner than any of the rest of us.*

### DANIEL REESE

Like Grace, he was busy—busy all the time—and runs came from his bat at a rate that made the score mount rapidly.

Captain E W Ballantine, the noted South African cricket journalist and chronicler of 100 Test matches, told me that he would go miles farther to see Bradman's fielding than he would to watch his scoring a century.

### W RHODES

The wonderful and untiring eye of Donald Bradman and his brilliant footwork, together with his superb self-confidence made it possible for him to accomplish the record-breaking performances . . .

Bradman can go straight to the wicket and start scoring at once, and all the time he is batting he looks like continuing to score at the same even but rapid pace.

## V Y RICHARDSON

As a fieldsman in the deep he was the finest I have seen. His speed and anticipation were terrific and his throw was deadly.

## R C ROBERTSON-GLASGOW

Few, if any, had so disciplined themselves to physical excellence, or fielded and thrown with such agility or accuracy.

With a mind as keen and enduring as Toledo steel, a body that might have won a welter-weight boxing championship, and feet as nimble as Fred Astaire's, he answered the craving of the multitude to an almost inhuman degree.

Statistics cannot record the number of runs he carried with him to each innings. But, in a country of great fieldsmen, he stood out pre-eminent. His gathering and throwing approached perfection.

No one before had ever been quite so fit, quite so ruthless.

Further, enabling his execution, were a physical fitness and endurance rarely seen on the cricket field.

Like the few great, he saw the ball and its intentions very early, as they say; and he had the answer to spin or swerve, to fast or sticky pitches.

## RAY ROBINSON

His secret lay in peerless co-ordination of eyes, mind, feet and hands.

For rapid interception and high-velocity throwing he was in the first flight of outfielders.

I have never seen a quicker-moving batsman, nor one who could start his stroke later yet finish it on time . . .

There was something feverish in Bradman's brilliance. It was as if he had posted up one of those shop placards: Great Fire Sale. Everything Must Go.

## C F ROOT

### *His footwork would do credit to an expert dancer.*

## IRVING ROSENWATER

Whereas all other batsmen in the world seem to work for their runs, Bradman just stood there or rather moved his feet with lightning speed—and pulverised any attack.

He wrote a song entitled 'Every Day is a Rainbow Day for Me' that was introduced during the performance of the pantomine *Beauty and the Beast* at the Grand Opera House in Melbourne in February 1931.

He was chosen for local representative tennis tournaments and won at least one local championship.

As an athlete he won the 100 yards, 220 yards, 440 yards and 880 yards events at one and the same school athletic meeting.

The piano at Glebe Street gave Don Bradman much pleasure and his skill aspired to a more than ordinary standard. Even with jazz music he showed remarkable delicacy of touch.

Like his father, he was a good rifle shot.

He carried in his head telephone numbers and addresses of friends and all those small facts that most people put on paper. He was not only a remarkable cricketer!

### 'SECOND SLIP'

Methodical to a degree, with a lightning eye and excellent wrists, he was so quick on his feet that he was able to get well over the ball, seldom, if ever, lifting it off the ground . . .

### 'SHEFFIELD TELEGRAPH'

*People who have heard Don Bradman's public speeches since he arrived have been commenting on what a witty and pointed speaker he is.*

### 'SMITHS NEWSPAPERS'

His fair hair sparkled in the sunshine as he ran like a hare round the boundary to save fours . . .

### 'SMITHS WEEKLY'

Nerves of steel, grim determination, allied with keen eye, exquisite footwork and a spirit that is unconquerable; an incurable optimism that was once mistaken for braggadocio—these are the attributes of Bradman.

### S J SOUTHERTON

The number of potential fours he turned into singles in the Test match at the Oval was extraordinary.

Nothing during the whole tour could have been more dazzling than the manner in which at Leeds he threw Hobbs out from deep mid-off.

In match after match his work at deep mid-off and in the long-field was a joy to watch.

To an eye almost uncanny in its power to gauge the length of a ball was allied really beautiful footwork.

### H Sutcliffe

*He was the finest fielder and best thrower I have ever seen.*

### E W Swanton

The impression that remains is of the smooth, unhurried rhythm of his play. Bat and man seemed one, the ball persuaded by a marvellous precision of timing.

The stranger seeing him for the first time must have noticed the exceptional quickness of his reactions, his speed between the wickets and the lithe fitness that enabled him to take the longest innings in his stride.

### Graham Tarrant

His judgement, timing, footwork and concentration were in a class of their own, the runs flowing from his bat in all directions with a speed and certainty that drove bowlers almost to distraction.

### A A Thomson

If he had chosen to dedicate his unforgiving efficiency and ferocious determination to any other calling, he might have become Prime Minister of Australia at the very least.

*In its context, his batting was the modern machine-gun. It was the perfect co-ordination of hand and eye and feet with the quickest reflexes ever possessed by any cricketer.*

### F H Tyson

Bradman's inner fires, however, burned more fiercely than the normal, independently motivated sportsman.

Bradman, however, achieved such heights of concentration in the logical analysis of sport and business that he succeeded in exceptional terms in every task which he faced.

### R B Vincent

. . . and never overlook, in glorifying his scoring power, the immense amount of runs this glorious fieldsman has saved.

### W Voce

*Bradman was like a cat, he was so quick-footed. He would have to be No. 1 in an all-time XI.*

### J H B Waite

. . . Bradman could make the greatest bowling in the world his plaything, simply because his footwork converted each ball into the appropriate length for each type of stroke he wished to play.

### B J Wakley

Furthermore, he was one of the best fieldsmen ever to play for Australia.

## PAT WARD-THOMAS

He spoke so modestly that it was hard to believe that this was the man whose astoundingly swift reaction and movement had enabled him to plunder bowling as no man ever did.

And when Bradman is minded to do anything, no matter what, he excels at it. I was told that he was the best billiards player in Australia after Walter Lindrum . . .

## SIR PELHAM WARNER

It is strikingly apparent how absolutely still Bradman stands until the ball is halfway down the pitch. Then follows a lightning movement of his feet and bat, and the ball crashes into the crowd.

Indeed, I think he is the quickest batsman on his feet I have ever seen.

Apart from his phenomenal feats with the bat, Bradman has stood out as the finest out-fieldsman in England.

. . . and I think that he should present his boots to the Australian nation, to be placed in the pavilion at Sydney, there to be kept in a glass case for future generations to gaze on, and to inspire them to something like his own nimbleness of foot.

Never have I seen anyone move forward faster to the ball, pick it up more quickly, or throw it harder.

Bradman looked every inch a cricketer. He was scrupulously neat and smart in his turn-out, and he played the game with rare zest and enjoyment.

So much for his batting—but he was also a long field of the very highest class, quick to start, a fast runner, and the possessor of a return as swift as an arrow from a bow, and full pitch into the wicket-keeper's hands.

### ERIC WHITEHEAD

The recently retired Australian wizard of the willow attains a unique stature among athletes.

### R S WHITINGTON

As a fielder he was amongst the greatest of any era . . .

Nobody can remember him disputing any umpire's decision.

Under direction from these attributes were an armoury of strokes to which the swiftest of footwork and the quintessence of timing gave astonishing precision and power.

Bradman appeared to see and judge each delivery earlier than any other player, and his speed of eye and decision was matched by the mercury in his feet.

### R W E WILMOT

*Temperament is the only word to describe just everything that surrounds Bradman and his cricket. In momentary failure, in success, he still remains, after a most eventful season, the laughing boy, the run-maker, the inventor of new strokes, the best batsman in the world.*

The best illustration of temperament I know is the case of Don Bradman. In him it is developed to the $n$th degree. It possesses him, radiates from him, raises him above his fellows in the most remarkable way.

### 'WISDEN CRICKETERS' ALMANACK'

Bradman—best of my time. He was also the best fielder I have seen. During a Test, no batsman scored more than a single from a ball placed anywhere near him.

Over and above his batting he is a magnificent field and, like all Australians, a beautiful thrower.

### W M WOODFULL

Some of his strokes were positively cheeky, but still remained brilliant in an amazing combination of footwork and superb timing.

### R E S WYATT

He was able to judge the length of a ball exceptionally early in its flight, which enabled him to play strokes which others wouldn't even attempt.

### N YARDLEY

. . . a great cricketer and a very great sportsman.

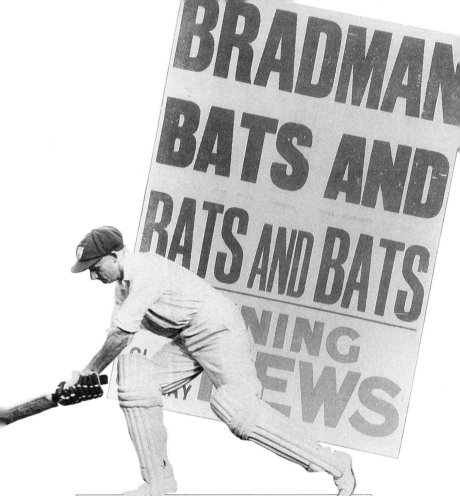

## THE COLOSSUS
### One Scarcely Ventures to Speak of Him

❛Don Bradman has made so much
cricket history of the marvellous sort that
one scarcely ventures to speak of him.❜

EDMUND BLUNDEN

## L ARMARNATH

He is not only a great batsman, he is a great and charming personality.

## L E G AMES

*If he came back today, he'd be streets ahead of anyone else.*

## JOHN ARLOTT

Don Bradman, as a public figure, has taken seriously his duty to the public.

From late April until September 1948, in England, Donald George Bradman played cricket, captained a cricket team, made speeches, was polite to bores, ignored the spite of those who begrudged him what he had earned, kept his temper and consolidated a great public reputation.

I feel he is capable of such single-minded concentration as to be able to achieve almost anything within his physical compass with utter competence and with an intensity rare in the human race.

He is far more than a cricketer; he has been a celebrity wherever he has gone, but his own country sees him as something more than that.

## T E BAILEY

. . . but of all batsmen he is the one I would most like to have on my side.

## E H M BAILLIE

He is unquestionably the greatest run-getter that the game

has known, and scores almost as freely from the best bowling as he does from the weakest.

Don Bradman's feat of making 100 centuries in first-class cricket is one that can never be equalled by an Australian batsman for a great many years, if it is ever equalled.

### ERIC BARBOUR

*Bradman has a cricket mentality that is at his age nothing short of colossal.*

### S G BARNES

. . . he was the uncrowned king of Australian cricket and I was only too eager to listen to any advice he gave me.

Much better I thought to get in before him than to come later, like flat beer after champagne.

### SIR JAMES BARRIE

Bradman, when you were here before, we knew that another prodigy had arisen in the land of cricket.

### PERCY BEAMES

With a memorable 172 against the Indians, Don Bradman, Australia's greatest run-getting machine, made history by being the first player, outside English country cricket, to score 100 centuries in first-class cricket.

### A V BEDSER

. . . the most amazing batsman of all time . . .

Bowlers used to win the matches, but Sir Donald Bradman, from 1930 to 1949 (with one exception) tore the theory to shreds.

## A J Bell

> *Consequently, when Don comes in nobody knows where to stand; they pray fervently that either he'll get out, or that six o'clock will hurry up.*

Another remarkable thing about Bradman is that he never seems to perspire. Our bowlers used to get through three or four shirts a day, but Don comes out in an immaculate silk shirt at noon and at six o'clock is still in an immaculate silk shirt.

## Ben Bennison

To the last ounce he knew his value, not only as a cricketer but as a man . . .

## Sir William Norman Birkett

He is already in the company of the very greatest cricketers of any age or clime.

## 'Birmingham Post'

'Colossal' seems the only epithet for such a cricketer as D G Bradman. And how young a Colossus! While still but 21 he bestrides our English grounds with batsmanship of a stature which even the most bigoted *laudator temporis acti* must confess to be gigantic.

## Edmund Blunden

Don Bradman has made so much cricket history of the marvellous sort that one scarcely ventures to speak of him.

## W E Bowes

Greatest cricketer of all . . . Don Bradman.

### CHARLES BRAY

It is not necessary to enumerate his deeds. They are written in letters of gold in the records.

### TERRY BRINDLE

*A new Bradman? Slater would rather sling a deadweight around his neck and step off the Harbour Bridge. It would be a quicker and less painful route into one form of immortality.*
*(Brindle on Michael Slater)*

### AUSTEN BROWN

Undoubtedly he is the greatest batsman of all time.

. . . and as long as cricketers gather to talk of the king of sports Don's name will be honoured . . .

### FRANK BROWNE

. . . the game had never seen anything like him before as a batsman or a captain.

### ALEX BUZO

Bowlers were second-guessed and checkmated by the most successful batsman in the history of cricket. It was almost as if Bradman had been given a start in life.

Don Bradman challenged many Australian myths. He worked hard and did better than anyone else; he took things seriously, and he was an elitist by instinct if not in practice.

### H B CAMERON

*He's enough to break your heart—the perfect batsman.*

### SIR NEVILLE CARDUS

There is no argument about the name of the game's greatest match-winning stroke player when Bradman is Bradman.

I firmly believe that throughout his career most bowlers would have supported any legal means whereby, before a match, Bradman could have been bought off, or compounded with, by the gift of 100 runs on condition that he did not bat.

He will in the end find himself regarded not so much a master batsman, but as a phenomenon of cricket.

Again the matter boils down to Bradman. O'Reilly is a great bowler, the only living great bowler, but he could not have saved his side. Bradman, always Bradman.

This was the Bradman of my heart's desire, and whenever I write critically of his play it is when he forgets his genius and trusts to talent.

He always knew what was within his power and would, without boastfulness, face a heavy responsibility as though it had presented itself merely to be set aside.

### CLIF CARY

*It is in the highest degree unlikely that many of Bradman's records will ever be broken. Statistically he is assured of immortality.*

### FRANK CHESTER

I left the Lord's Test in 1930, after watching Bradman, firmly convinced that he was the greatest batsman of all time.

### D C S COMPTON

. . . a batsman appearing not just once in a lifetime but once in the life of a game.

## LORD CONSTANTINE

Stories grow round Don like barnacles round a ship. There may be batsmen who score as many runs, some future day, but there will never be another like this one.

## M C COWDREY

Inevitably he is at his most dazzling on the subject of cricket. He has the sharpest cricket mind of all the cricketers I have met.

The quite reckless ability to drive himself, to concentrate utterly, to exhaust any problem he thought worthy of his attention, to waste no time on fools and frivolity, to live his life to meticulous schedules, made him the remarkable cricketer he was and the extraordinary man he is.

## ROBERT CRADDOCK

... Bradman stood out like King Kong at a jockeys' reunion.

## BRIAN CROWLEY

'The Don' was, at all stages of his career, the undisputed champion of all time.

## 'DAILY HERALD'

This match, however, has revealed the world's most wonderful batsman for all time.

## 'DAILY MAIL'

Bradman was a mountain among molehills.

A more level-headed young man or one less likely to become spoiled by admiration never wore flannels.

## KEN DALBY

*Bradman was not content to repeat history, he embellished it.*

## ANTHONY DAVIS

. . . your personal charm, courtesy, good fellowship and complete efficiency and modesty in everything you have undertaken have done much to make cricket the vital force it is today . . .

## J C DAVIS

*He's a team in himself.*

## H A DE LACY

There were Larwood, Verity, Woodfull, Constantine, Headley, Ponsford, O'Reilly, Grimmett and Amar Singh. Each has his own niche in fame. But great as they were, none ever reached the heights attained by Bradman.

Though small in stature, he stepped among the giants as a breathtaking colossus.

## PHILIP DERRIMAN

There has been none like him. Most Australians, I think, have given up hoping there ever will be.

## E W DOCKER

. . . what was indisputably true was that Bradman had emerged as the cricket phenomenon of his age . . .

## SIDNEY DOWNER

. . . spectators, still rumbling and unrepenting, saw an

innings which for virtuosity, agility, courage, and inventiveness has rarely been witnessed at the Adelaide Oval.

### W J Edrich

A batsman so supremely great, so much above his contemporaries, was bound to be the mark of every Test bowler, the particular study of every fieldsman, the cynosure of all Press cameras, the flashpoint of cricket criticism . . .

### T G Evans

*It was that man again—Don Bradman . . . I realised that all I had heard about this amazing little Australian was true.*

### H V Evatt

He has the extremely rare quality of cricket imagination and employs it scientifically.

### 'Evening News' *(headline)*

## BRADMAN
## BATS AND
## BATS AND BATS

### Ernest Eytle

. . . Sir Donald Bradman walked down the steps of the Oval in London to play his last Test innings, and Norman Yardley, the English skipper, marshalled his men for three rousing cheers as the great man made his way to the wicket. There had been a solemnity in that homage, a very English, restrained farewell to the greatest cricketer of his age; a batsman feared by his opponents and admired the world over for the skill and mastery he had exercised at the crease.

### KENNETH FARNES

Bradman is a model of modern efficiency.

### P G H FENDER

Bradman is capable of winning almost any match off his own bat . . .

### J H FINGLETON

In all this adulation, in all this hero worshipping, which came at its flood when he had just passed his 21st birthday, Bradman never lost his balance.

Together with all other cricketers of our generaton, I salute him as the greatest player of his age, the greatest attraction the game of cricket has known.

### ANDY FLANAGAN

As a cricketer he defies comparison.

### C B FRY

It is a simple point: modern giants play at the ball as they figure it will come. This little master plays at the ball as it is. The difference between mastery and mediocrity—with the bat.

### ALAN GIBSON

Besides, Bradman was Bradman, the greatest player of his time.

The only other great batsman of whom this might be said is Ranjitsinhji, but Ranji's career to Bradman's was a shooting star to a comet. Bradman was *sui generis.*

### A E R Gilligan

. . . I can honestly say that in my cricketing life I have never seen anyone to equal Don Bradman. He will always occupy first place in my estimation.

. . . in 1946 it was worth travelling 12 000 miles to see Australia's great artist compile his 234 in the second Test match at Sydney.

### Mark Gosling

Bradman is the Phar Lap of cricket. Mr Lang and Mr Lyons are looking at new taxation schemes, and I would suggest that they might impose a tax on centuries, and make Don pay a super-tax on every second century.

### Benny Green

*A career average of 99.94 smacks less of reality than of the cloud-cuckoo-land of the tuppenny bloods . . .*

### W R Hammond

*If I were choosing a side out of all the cricketers who have ever lived, I would put Bradman's name down first. None of us had the measure of him and that's the plain fact.*

### Joe Hardstaff

Other cricketers have achieved great fame, but none has been quite so famous. Don Bradman stands apart from other cricketers . . .

## BRUCE HARRIS

His fifties seem to the popular mind as ten from other men; not until he approaches the 200 is his innings counted normal.

## LORD HARRIS

The better side won. Bradman is a cricket phenomenon. We have nothing like him.

## R N HARVEY

Bradman's ability as a batsman was something even a fairy-tale hero couldn't rival.

## V HAZARE

Sir Donald Bradman . . . I have not see a better batsman at the crease.

## GEORGE HELE

But, in my opinion, and into it enters not a shadow of a doubt, Sir Donald Bradman was the greatest of all the batsmen I have watched—the most valuable and devastating batsman any Test team of any country ever owned.

## E H HENDREN

Some of the Test match records with which his name has been associated may stand for all time.

## H J HENLEY

*He dwarfed all other batsmen as much by the attractiveness of his style as by the size of his scores.*

## C HILL

Bradman is the greatest batsman in the world at present.

Congratulations, you little devil, for breaking my record.

I saw Macartney at Leeds in 1926, and said he surpassed Trumper. Bradman is Trumper and Macartney at their best rolled into one.

## SIR JACK HOBBS

I can only describe Bradman as a freak batsman.

Whatever odds there may be on any other player getting a score, those odds are increased by 50 per cent when Don walks to the crease.

## BERNARD HOLLOWOOD

Bradman hits too many runs to be universally popular. He made so many runs that he was always at the wicket often when his colleagues were at the bar.

## VIVIAN JENKINS

If Grace put cricket on the map, Bradman held it there, and made it glow with incandescent heat. What a man, and what a record.

## I W JOHNSON

He was the maestro.

### James A Jones

*Bradman makes his century, as he was bound to do from the very start. We gave him a cheer. So do the Englishmen. Then we lean forward once more, and watch with strained eyes.*

### J M Kilburn

To contain him it would have been necessary to institute a different concept.

For Bradman, Headingley offered a glorious beginning, continuation and finale. He played six Test match innings there and his scores were 334, 304, 103, 16, 33, and 173 not out.

### J C Laker

Bradman was the greatest player I have ever seen or played against.

### H Larwood

You hear talk that modern day batsmen like Greg Chappell are as good as Bradman . . . Chappell would not be in the same street, nor would any other Australian or batsmen from any other country since the war.

### R R Lindwall

*. . . everything is bound to work out right, 'the Don' is playing.*

### C G Macartney

Bradman has thoroughly earned his reputation as the champion.

## ALAN MCGILVRAY

Don Bradman has always been, and undoubtedly always will be, the ultimate talent by which succeeding generations of batsmen are measured.

Nobody will ever touch Bradman. He was one apart.

His manner won him a different kind of respect. There was an aura about Bradman.

He remained a very private person, and he wanted it kept that way.

## A A MAILEY

Among the prominent regular players the amazing Bradman still stands head and shoulders above his team mates.

## A A MALLETT

To my mind Bradman stands head and shoulders above the rest.

## JOHN MARSHALL

Bradman, the magnificent, hit 304 against England at Leeds and finished the tour with seven centuries behind him and a Test average of 94.75.

## CHRISTOPHER MARTIN-JENKINS

The most famous and illustrious cricketer in the world, he was, after all, hot property.

## H H MASSIE

He's a champion. There's no doubt about that.

### P J Millard

*Now, amid ringing applause from the whole cricketing world, the greatest batsman and most dynamic personality in the history of the game, and regarded as one of the two best-known men in the Empire (Churchill being the other) finally puts away his bat . . .*

### P J Moss

He is the greatest run-getting machine playing cricket, and I doubt if a greater has ever taken part in the series.

### A G Moyes

You simply can't rank anyone ahead of him.

In compiling 100 centuries in 295 first-class innings, Bradman created a record which almost certainly will never be beaten.

Bradman has been—and still is—a world figure. It is fitting that the honour achieved yesterday [100 centuries] should go to one so worthy to hold it, not merely as a batsman, but as a man and citizen.

### Patrick Murphy

*'Body-line' was born for the 1932/33 series. It was specifically designed to bring down Bradman to the status of ordinary mortals and it remains the greatest compliment ever paid to one player.*

When considering the batting record of Sir Donald George Bradman, it is almost impossible to still a sense of wonder.

### 'NEWS AND CHRONICLE'

We must acclaim Bradman as the greatest batsman of the age. Maybe in a few years he will be recognised as the greatest of any age.

### W J O'REILLY

He was on his own. Nobody these days could live with him.

### MICHAEL PAGE

Regardless of how much longer his career was to endure, he had joined the immortals of the ancient game.

### H A PAWSON

*Arguments about who is the best batsman in history are a pointless charade: Bradman is not only the best, he leaves the rest of the field out of sight.*

### IAN PEEBLES

From the first glimpse there could be no doubt of the altogether exceptional quality of this new phenomenon.

The remarkable decade just before the war will ever be famous amongst cricketers as the Bradman era, for no individual since W G had so much influence on the game as 'the Don'.

### JACK POLLARD

Bradman was the Australian embodiment of the American democratic romance—from log cabin to the White House— a country lad who seized his chance.

While Australians had been a people willing to be led, a race sadly convinced of its inferiority, but now there was hope that in some fields at least they could take on the world.

### DANIEL REESE

. . . but it was not until the arrival of Donald Bradman that Australians and Englishmen alike acclaimed in him another 'first equal' who had won the right to rank with Grace.

### W RHODES

You can have any cricketer you care to mention, but I'll take Bradman—he's the best by a long chalk.

Frankly, I do not know which is the most remarkable feature about this very remarkable young man . . .

### TIM RICE

He is quite simply the greatest run-maker the game has ever known.

### V Y RICHARDSON

His figures in Test matches alone read like some cricketing fable . . .

### ANTON RIPPON

*They say there are lies, damned lies, and statistics; but Bradman's figures tell their own tale without further comment.*

### E L ROBERTS

When an individual is known to his or her contemporaries or posterity merely by a surname, it is safe to assume that such a person has achieved lasting fame.

## R C ROBERSTON-GLASGOW

Like his fellow-countryman Walter Lindrum in billiards, he sought and achieved a numerical standard not previously contemplated.

Like a second W G Grace he has changed the conception of first-class batting, opening avenues hitherto untrodden, suggesting possibilities till now unsuspected.

We feel we have a share in him. He is more than Australian. He is a world batsman.

Never was such ambition achieved and sustained . . . To set such a standard was unique. To keep it was a miracle.

. . . in Australia, in 1938/39, he scored 801 runs at an average of 160.2. All other modern cricketers may 'with a blush retire'.

No single player, not W G himself, has ever so nearly approached to being the sole hinge of victory. He was not only the champion of Australia; he was almost Australia itself.

. . . his fame will last as long as there is cricket.

## RAY ROBINSON

*If the countless columns and chapters published about Bradman were placed end to end, they would stretch, on a still day, from the pavilion end to Puckapunyal, and would reach beyond the bounds of credibility.*

His successes are enough to make a United States communique seem like an understatement.

## IRVING ROSENWATER

Who else could score 100 runs in three overs? Who else could pass a triple-century on the first day of an England–Australia Test? Who else could score a century every third time he went to the wicket in his first-class career? Who else could score 7000 runs in less than a year? Who else, on no less than 27 occasions in first-class cricket alone, could score 200 runs in a single day off his own bat? Who else could average 99.94 in a Test career spanning 20 years?

By the mid-1930s Don Bradman was of course many things to many people. To the bowler, he was cricket's greatest menace; to the spectator, he was cricket's greatest spectacle; and to the game's treasurers he was undoubtedly cricket's greatest money spinner.

He did not have bad patches and he did not have bad luck.

. . . and when he took his score to 200 next day he became—as he still is—the youngest Australian to make a double-century in England, three weeks younger than Trumper.

It had been easy for the writers to go overboard, but there had been nothing like Don Bradman on the sporting scene in all their experience.

The increased practice of record-keeping, fanned into a journalistic and public pastime directly through Don Bradman's record-breaking, served further to push Bradman high up the scale and to push other batsmen lower down it.

### J RYDER

A marvel and greatest batsman in the world today. His stamina, his mental outlook, his quickness on his feet, and his other qualities all contribute to his greatness. There is no telling how far he will go.

### JACK SCOTT

I never thought I would see anyone better than Trumper or Macartney but Bradman is the greatest batsman Australia has ever produced.

### J A SEITZ

He is an ornament as a captain, as a cricketer and as a man and thoroughly deserves this honour. He has done so much for cricket.

*(on Bradman's knighthood)*

### IVAN SHARPE

| *His record is astonishing—unbelievably great.* |

### 'SMITHS NEWSPAPERS'

When some unborn star makes 300 runs in a Test match in the year 2005 the cricket writers of the day will turn back the book of records and write—with authority: 'Great as today's performance was, it still fails to beat the world's Test record established by the Australian, Don Bradman, at Leeds away back in 1930.'

### S J SOUTHERTON

Nothing like his series of colossal innings in Test matches had ever before been witnessed.

### EDWARD STOKES

In the Tests played in his 39th and 40th years Bradman totalled 1903 runs, at an averageof 105.72—surely an unsurpassable finale to an unparalleled career.

### 'SUN'

Mussolini, Charles Chaplin and Fritz Kreisler now have nothing on Bradman . . .

### 'SYDNEY MORNING HERALD'

Who did the lion's share towards this great money-making tour? Bradman. He has done more here for cricket since his four years of first-class play than the Board has done since it was formed.

Bradman is still breaking and making records. Soon only his own will be left.

### GEOFFREY TEBBUTT

Bradman cannot be compared with any other great batsman.

### GEORGE THATCHER

Hats off to Don Bradman, greatest Australian run-getter . . .

### A A THOMSON

Bradman broke nearly every known record and set up more records that will never be broken.

You could describe this second 300 at Leeds by many adjectives beginning with an *m*: for the spectator who hoped for one little flaw in infallibility, monotonous; and for the bowler whose figures were round about none for 150, monstrous.

. . . there were more players who came closer to the Old Man's beard than ever came anywhere near to the level of Bradman's firm chin.

On his first English visit, in 1930, his aggregate in all Tests was 976, the highest total ever made or likely to be made by a human being with a bat in his hands.

With the 1934 tour he was back on top of the world and never abdicated from his throne.

If the hero of a sporting novel had been credited with a mere half of Bradman's scores, the publisher would have taken the author and murmured 'Come, come, my boy, plausibility, plausibility, if you please . . .'.

Is there any doubt about Bradman's imperial rule? Nobody before him, except W G Grace, and nobody at all since, has so toweringly bestridden the world of cricket as Bradman dominated it.

The incredible is Bradman, who for 20 years bestrode our petty world like a colossus.

### 'THE TIMES'

It was in fact an innings so glorious that it might be well classed as incomparable . . .

Australia takes the Ashes, and Bradman, her bright particular star, most of the new records.

King George V had been able to see an innings which would be destined to be famous as long as the game exists.

. . . no player, since history was made in the Hambledon era on Windmill Down, has contributed more to the game.

### UNKNOWN NEWSPAPER

*The cricketing colossus, as well he might be called, leaves behind a tally of records never likely to be broken in the game as we know it today.*

### B J WAKLEY

He is certainly the most consistently successful batsman to play cricket, and one of the very greatest, his run-getting performances, against all classes of bowling, both in Australia and England, and for over 20 years, being quite extraordinary.

### SIR PELHAM WARNER

*I believe Bradman would make a hundred in a blackout.*

Whatever comparisons may be drawn between him and other great batsmen past or present, there surely can never have been a greater batsman.

### TOM WEBSTER

By the time Bradman has finished telling us that he likes tea, cricket, milk, money, music, tinsel paper and the gramophone it ought to be close of play—and close of play is, I think, the only way to get rid of Mr Bradman.

### E M WELLINGS

His tally of runs, his number of centuries, and his complete mastery of the opposing attack have been without parallel.

## PERCY WESTBROOK

He has made a conquest of himself; his head is not turned; he returns to us unspoiled and unmoved by public glamour and behind it all is the respect he holds for his mother and his home.

## R S WHITINGTON

*When Hitler's war broke out Bradman was given 21 lines in* Who's Who—*eight fewer than Hitler, 17 more than Stalin.*

No one man has come as close to controlling an era of Test cricket as he did from 1930 until his retirement in 1948.

If, as has been claimed, there will never be another Trumper, there is even less likelihood that there will be another Bradman.

## TREVOR WIGNALL

I can easily remember such stars as Spooner, Ranjitsinhji, Trumper, and others of the truly great, but none of them was better than this astonishing boy from a hamlet in Australia.

. . . the most sensible way to refer to him now is by stating that he is Don Bradman, which merely means that he occupies a niche of his own.

## 'WISDEN CRICKETERS' ALMANACK'

When it is considered that Bradman made his first appearance in a big match only just over three years ago—to be exact it was at Adelaide in December 1927—his rise to the very top of the tree has been phenomenal.

Against South Africa, however, he showed brilliant form and accomplished a feat unparalleled in Australian cricket by making seven centuries in successive matches.

### W M WOODFULL

*If I were a selector I should count him as two batsman if he was playing in form. I mean that literally.*

## THE GENIUS
### ...a Very Hard Act to Follow

*‛Bradman was a very hard act to follow. Such was his genius that it appears improbable that the game will ever see his like again.’*

F H TYSON

## H S Altham

In many pictures that I have stored in my mind from the 'burnt-out-Junes' of 40 years, there is none more dramatic or compelling than that of Bradman's small, serenely moving figure in its big-peaked green cap coming out of the pavilion shadows into the sunshine, with the concentration, ardour and apprehension of surrounding thousands centred upon him, and the destiny of a Test match in his hands.

Genius defies analysis, but no one can watch a long innings by Bradman without realising some of his outstanding assets . . .

And of this game, with its happy associations and its reflections of so much that we hold worthwhile, Don Bradman is the unchallenged champion.

## John Arlott

Records, captaincy, an immense record of wins and a knighthood, all have come Bradman's way through the game he mastered with single-minded concentration.

## Oscar Asche

*Come, Bradman, rise, strike out,*
*belittlers stun;*
*By fresh deeds prove you are still*
*Don—not done.*

## T E Bailey

Gary [Sobers] admires him enormously—as a person, as the greatest batsman of all time, and for his exceptional knowledge of the game.

## E H M BAILLIE

Cricket enthusiasts will argue as to whether Don Bradman is or is not the greatest batsman of all time, but there can be no argument as to the amazing character of his batting since he entered first-class cricket in 1927/28.

## K F BARRINGTON

. . . a genius, in a class of his own . . .

## DR KEITH BARRY

Whilst hundreds of people searched for Don Bradman the night of his record innings, that musical youth sat in solitary splendour, and refreshed his tired limbs and brain by playing a gramophone and whistling.

## DENZIL BATCHELOR

The great Don—he served cricket well.

Once again the game resolved itself into Bradman versus All England. This Adelaide innings was the champagne of batsmanship.

## A V BEDSER

*If genius is the art of doing the simple things properly, Bradman was a classic example.*

## R BENAUD

'The Don'—head of the world's family of batsmen.

A remarkable man—I have no doubt he has always been a remarkable man . . .

. . . but it was the speed of his reflexes that was at the heart of his genius.

### REV R BIRCH HOYLE

To see perfection in any art is a joy to the soul. We saw the perfect artistry of the world's greatest batsman. Even as a study in psychology the innings was a gem. Four crashing strokes to the boundary signalled his arrival at the wicket.

### SIR WILLIAM NORMAN BIRKETT

. . . to remember Bradman, emerging from the Pavilion at Lord's on a June evening to enthrall the mighty crowd with an innings of supreme beauty . . .

It was once said that 'nothing in this world is precious until we know that it will soon be gone', but that was never true of the batting and the fielding of Mr Bradman.

### W E BOWES

He was not merely head and shoulders above all other batsmen, he was better almost from the ankles up.

### G BOYCOTT

Bradman, a genius and twice as good as any other batsman . . .

### GEORGE BRADMAN *(father)*

I would describe his batting as practically a freak. There is no other term which adequately describes it.

### LADY BRADMAN

I have never been more than a little apprehensive. His calmness always inspired me with confidence.

### MRS E BRADMAN *(mother)*

Although I am so proud of him—and what mother would

not be?—I am not the least afraid of his success turning his head as it might do with most young fellows.

His scores are amazing, and as they follow one after another I can hardly realise that it is my boy who is being acclaimed as one of the greatest cricketers in the world.

### CHARLES BRAY

To write an appreciation of Don Bradman as a cricketer is rather like praising perfection, for this slim, sharp-featured, self-centred Australian has proved himself to be king of them all.

### AUSTEN BROWN

*My firm belief is that none of us will ever see his equal again.*

### MRS LYDIA CAMPBELL *(an 85-year-old fan)*

I've seen him, and I think he is just as wonderful as a boy as he is a cricketer, and I would like to tell his mother that.

### SIR NEVILLE CARDUS

He beggared description and achievement.

His genius has its own logic and authority. Apparently he is free to play off any foot, and transform into greatness and grandeur what in other players would be errors fatal and unlovely. There is the gamin about him somehow.

Cricketers in England will rejoice that the last rays of Bradman's splendour will fall on the greatest fields in the world.

I wonder if Bradman ever grows tired of his own mastery and sighs for new worlds to conquer, new reaches of achievement outside the great capacity of his skill.

A newspaper column couldn't contain him. He was, as far as a cricketer can be, a genius.

Perhaps by making a duck some day, Bradman will oblige those of his critics who believe, with Lord Bacon, that there should always be some strangeness, something unexpected, mingled with art and beauty.

I could not take my eyes off Bradman for a second. My heart was beating as I saw his bat go back so masterfully, so grandly.

### CLIF CARY

He was a star with ten extras . . .

### G S CHAPPELL

There is no comparison between what Sir Donald did in 50 odd Tests and what some other bloke may have done in 80 odd. It would be almost sacrilegious to pass him.

*(on approaching Bradman's 6996 Test runs)*

### 'CHRISTIAN RENEWAL'

**Bradman is living witness to the very important truth that men are not equal.**

### D C S COMPTON

His like will not be seen again, and I count it as my privilege that I was able to study his technique and methods from the closeness of slip and gully.

But 'the Don' is no ordinary batsman but a genius . . .

### CLAUDE CORBETT

The story of how a country lad of 21 years, unknown four years ago, burst through into the great national game of the British Empire, and in a few short seasons forever emblazoned his name on the scroll of cricket fame.

He today was the three Musketeers rolled into one, debonair, full of life, afraid of nothing . . .

### GERRY COTTER

The supply of superlatives needed to describe his batting has long since run out . . .

### 'THE COURIER MAIL'

. . . in the minds of reminiscent cricket lovers the Bradman legend is just beginning to take on heroic shape and colour.

### 'CRICKETER'

Sir Donald Bradman's career has been analysed, dissected, investigated and considered by a whole multitude of commentators since the boy genius first burst on the cricket world over 30 years ago.

### A C M CROOME

To do justice to D Bradman's batting it is necessary to use the language of superlatives and compare it with the acting of Miss Marie Tempest. Both are so exquisitely right in the general design and the polished execution of every detail.

### BRIAN CROWLEY

*Bradman was an unchallenged, unorthodox genius who became a legend in his own life.*

### 'DAILY EXPRESS'

In young Bradman at Lord's, the genius of cricket yesterday was incarnate.

### 'DAILY MAIL'

Bradman is the boy wonder of cricket. His gigantic innings, following previous scores, shows his consistency and his genius.

### J DARLING

Bradman has undoubtedly proved to be the world's greatest batsman. He has the right temperament and the stamina. He is a cricket marvel and a genius.

### ANTHONY DAVIS

Nobody could have foretold that Don would come to be recognised by most people as the world's greatest cricketer—a genius of the game . . .

### J C DAVIS

His skill is so transcending that his brilliant career has been studded with record-breaking achievements.

### PHILIP DERRIMAN

No, the reason for Bradman's enduring appeal is surely the same as it has always been: his very uniqueness, his defiance of comparison.

### CHRISTOPHER DOUGLAS

*Fortunately, a quantity of newsreel footage showing the young Bradman still exists. Viewed in short clips and from a distance of 50 years, his every movement seems sheer grace;*

> *it is as if the bat is making the strokes and Bradman is following with his hands and feet in perfect sympathy.*

### SIDNEY DOWNER

. . . that amalgam of confidence, patience, daring, quickness of foot and eye—and something else to which he alone has the secret. Call it genius, call it something more prosaic but, whatever it is, it is all Bradman's.

### H V EVATT

Unique as his record is, it cannot adequately describe his genius.

### W H FERGUSON

I can pay him no greater compliment than to say I have seen Don Bradman . . . and I have seen other batsmen.

### J H FINGLETON

On and on and on he seemed to go, batting into cricket eternity.

He was the genius absolute.

There comes a time when the Pavilion swallows up all players for the last time, but the thousands at Lord's did not comprehend that Bradman would come no more. That seemed unbelievable.

### BILLY FINLAY

He showed in many ways that he is a cricket genius . . .

## LEO FITZGERALD

. . . I am sure there has never [been] and will never be a man of greater integrity and modesty.

## C B FRY

*The crack of his bat against the ball is proper music for man.*

I wish I could remember myself as a rival worthy of your competitive blade, but you have added so much to the novelty and complexity of stroke-play as well as to the standard and size of individual scores that none of us old-timers can regard himself even as a figurative rival.

Here is a master. He paid the price of struggle and has achieved success extraordinary.

## SIR GEORGE FULLER

I saw the whole of Bradman's innings at Lord's—it was a masterpiece.

## A G GARDINER

But there floats before the mental vision a slight athletic figure at the wicket that seems not a man but a whirlwind, a natural element that is more than human, and I am left wondering, 'Who is to get Bradman out?'

He has upset the balance of the game as it has never been upset before by the genius of a single player.

## ALAN GIBSON

Bradman, in the lengthening perspective of cricket history, will surely be seen as a spectactular eruption.

## BENNY GREEN

. . . *Wisden*, with an air of finality, published the full figures of the most amazing batting career in the history of the game.

## J GREGORY

*What can anyone say about Don? His innings was such a marvellous one that words can hardly express one's opinion of it. Well—it's just Don Bradman.*

## F J C GUSTARD

Bradman is a law unto himself, literally capable of winning a match off his own bat, and any suggestion that he could be for any length of time uneasy against any type of bowling can have no real foundation in fact.

## W R HAMMOND

On one or two occasions, when he was well set, and when he saw me move a fieldsman, he would raise his hand to me in mock salute, and then hit the next ball exactly over the place from which the man had just been moved. Reluctantly I had to admit once more that he was out of the ordinary run of batsmen—a genius.

But he will indeed be the marvel of marvels of the cricket world, past, present, and future . . .

## JOE HARDSTAFF

Bradman set his goal at the highest of all stars and he reached his goal. In setting such a high standard he achieved his ambition: to keep up the high standard was genius.

### LORD HARRIS

The boy, Bradman, is a marvellous and great cricketer.

### MAX HARRIS

His genius was to be able to read the bowler and then read the ball at high speed.

### V S HAZARE

We had read a great deal about Bradman's achievements and stories which pictured him as the greatest batsman on earth.

### C HILL

Bradman, after his 254 in the Lord's Test, was described by me as a marvel. He has now gone past that, and all I can say is that he is a marvellous marvel, or an LBW—'a living blooming wonder'.

What to say about Bradman is beyond me.

### SIR JACK HOBBS

*I recall that we said 'Well played' to him so often—'Well played, Bradman, well played, Don!'—that it became really monotonous!*

### SIR LEN HUTTON

But Bradman was Bradman, unique, a cricketer beyond comparison, and with deep reserves of character to support his talents.

### R ILLINGWORTH / KENNETH GREGORY

One aspect of Bradman's genius may be expressed in figures; the sheer and abiding wonder of his batting over 20 years is now only a cherished memory of those who saw him.

### C L R J A M E S

His excellences were multifarious and unique.

### C H A P M A N  J O C O S E

*So much has been written about Bradman that no superlatives are left. I said yesterday that he is a menace to English cricket. Today I go further. I think he will be the death of it. If he comes over more than once again, we shan't be able to spare the time to get him out, and English cricket will quietly fade away.*

### I W J O H N S O N

Before 'the Don' all others fade.

### R L J O N E S

There are no words in the English language wide enough to cover my opinion of Don. He's a wonder.

### J M K I L B U R N

He dominated and dazzled. He defied belief yet inflicted no outrage on cricketing logic or dignity.

Bradman's genius must have been based on physical attributes outside the ordinary.

I have seen Bradman clear, and would complete the illusion by saying I have seen him whole, except that I very much doubt if any one has ever seen Bradman whole because—as a cricketer, I mean—there is so much of him.

Wherever cricket lives, he will be discussed; dissected, perhaps decried, but never, never forgotten.

My belief is that he is beyond parallel.

## A F KIPPAX

*If Don played for the West Indies they would be the leading cricketing country. If he played for New Zealand they would be the leading cricketing country. If he played for England they would be the leading cricketing country. If he played for South Africa they would be the leading cricket country.*

## F G LAVERS

It was a matter of comparing brilliant unlike with brilliant unlike.

## ARCHIE LEDBROOKE

When Bradman came in it was a moment for the connoisseur.

## PHILIP LINDSAY

Don Bradman, like Shakespeare, like Dickens, like Rubens, gave me back my faith in the spirit of men . . .

. . . and that is why when I am in my bath-chair at Lord's or in Sydney I will be informing awed if sceptical youngsters that their heroes are no more than marionettes were they placed beside Don Bradman in his heyday . . .

Therefore, with all my heart, I write: Thank you, Don Bradman . . .

### ROBERT LYND

When Bradman came out of the pavillion with his bat, you could have guessed he was a man of genius even though you had never heard of him.

### G F McCLEARY

. . . under the Southern Cross a star of the first magnitude had arisen, and that upon its effulgence would largely depend the future destination of the Ashes.

### ALAN McGILVRAY

. . . a man whose deeds are so exceptional as to defy comparison.

### A A MAILEY

Bradman's innings was indescribable. The army of British overseas Pressmen were scratching their heads, trying to think of something new to say about Bradman.

His glorious innings stood out from those of his team mates like a diamond set in pieces of glass.

Bradman batted as though the wicket was perfect, but this dazzling fellow seemed to be so irrepressible that I believe he could have batted on a heap of stones.

### 'A MAN IN THE CROWD'

It was Bradman, Bradman all the way. It is almost impossible to describe his innings, because it was all of a piece. Any one period of it was just like any other. There was no crescendo, and very certainly no diminuendo; it was as eternal and spontaneous and delightful as a Bach fugue.

### RONALD MASON

At Lord's, before His Majesty King George V, Bradman revealed the power and extent of his genius. In two hours and forty minutes he made 155 without the ghost of a suspicion of a chance . . .

### JIM MATHERS

It is mere platitude to describe Bradman as a great batsman. Last year he was great. This year he is greater.

### SIR ROBERT MENZIES

For, mark you, Don Bradman is a man of uncommon intelligence, from whatever angle you consider him.

### FRANK MITCHELL

There are those who say that he cannot get any better, but when a genius or phenomenon of this nature crops up there is no telling what he may do.

### 'MONITOR BUREAU'

Next to Bradman comes nobody, so to speak, and then nobody, and then . . .

### CLARENCE MOODY

. . . a genius, who has developed 'the infinite capacity of taking pains' to a degree unequalled by any of his famous predecessors.

### 'MORNING POST'

All expectations have been confounded.

Bradman is a sort of reincarnation in miniature of Grace in his youthful prime.

## P J MOSS

I have had to describe Bradman's batting so often before
that one might think it superfluous to attempt it again.

## A G MOYES

I opened the door and a lad said: 'Are you Mr Moyes? I'm
Don Bradman!' Twelve years later I listened to this country
lad make speeches in England that were surely among the
finest ever made by a cricketer. I saw him lead Australia;
make centuries by the dozen, but the picture that remains is
that of the lad who said quietly: 'I'm Don Bradman.' His
name will live as long as cricket is played, and his glory will
never be blotted out.

His brilliance that day was like a flight of arrows in the sun.

In his batting he seems something more than mortal.

As Kingsford Smith thrills the world with the majesty of his
skill and organisation, so does Bradman compel our
admiration with his exceptional ability, resource and daring.

Bradman was the champion of all time. He set the fields
blazing with the burning heat of his genius.

No one can argue these figures. Bradman was unique.

. . . from tea onwards he was so brilliant that one could not
choose one gem, in particular, from a diadem of jewels.

Yesterday I watched him make his century of centuries, and
thought back of the years; not so much of his triumphs, but
of the manner in which he has borne his honours.

## Patrick Murphy

I have always felt that the statistical evaluation of his career has unfairly overshadowed his genius, his certainty of stroke-play, speed of scoring and impact on generations of cricket lovers.

His genius lay in the art of doing things simply, clinically and with phenomenal success.

## M A Noble

He does not take risks or give anything away, yet scores at an astonishing rate, revels in making runs, never tires of it, and is the marvel of the age.

## 'Not Out'

The ascendency of Don Bradman as a batsman is becoming more and more amazing.

## W A Oldfield

An amazing chap is Don! Gifted as he is with the attributes of greatness, he carries on in his quiet yet most determined way.

As my cricket associations with Bradman lengthen, I continue to discover new indications of mastery.

## W J O'Reilly

As a batsman, he was an undoubted genius.

Well, if I were a kid again and won the toss for first pick,
I'd take Bradman and give you the next three choices.
That's what I think of him as a cricketer.

Bradman, of course, I regarded as the greatest cricketer who
ever walked onto a ground.

### IAN PEEBLES

. . . he remains the greatest force of any cricket era . . .

. . . Bradman shone with sufficient brilliance to dispel any
doubts as to his supremacy.

### 'PICTORIAL'

Bradman is a cricketer of rarest genius, whose batting
combines the grace of a ballet dancer, with the forcefulness
of a blacksmith.

### KEN PIESSE

*Sir Donald George Bradman, 'the Don', is
regarded as the greatest cricketer of all,
the 'eighth wonder of the world'. His feats
are legendary.*

### WILLIAM POLLOCK

'Le Don' has played the great innings of the season. If there
is anything better to come from him or anyone else, may I
be there to see and share. The really great things of cricket
are treasures.

For more than 40 years I have watched great batsmen—
W G, Ranji, Trumper, Frank Woolley, Macartney, Jessop,
Hammond, Hobbs—and am grateful for many precious

hours from them, but never have I seen a masterpiece of batting more glorious than Don Bradman's 100.

An innings that thousands of us who love cricket are going to enshrine in our memories was played as the sun went down over Lord's on Saturday.

### W H PONSFORD

To compile such a colossal individual score (452 not out) in 415 minutes is a feat to marvel at.

### PRINCE OF WALES

How do you do it?

### DANIEL REESE

After a modest start in Test cricket, he soon became the most brilliant star on the horizon.

### W RHODES

I once saw him come in and put his first ball straight back past the bowler for four; and the second, and the third. He did it without getting his eye or anything. Yes, maybe Jack Hobbs second and Victor Trumper third, but Bradman first, without doubt . . .

You can have any cricketer you would like to mention, Fergie, but I'll take Bradman.

*(to W H Ferguson)*

### V Y RICHARDSON

There has never been anything like this, of course, before or since. Will there ever be anything like it again?

If the hero of some work of cricket fiction were made to do what Bradman actually did as a batsman, the book would be regarded as fantasy.

Looking back over almost 30 years, I still wonder more and more at his deeds. They increase rather than diminish in stature over the years.

Add his astute and single-minded leadership to his unparalleled batting and fielding ability, have regard to his telling contribution as an administrator, and you have the full picture of perhaps the most formidable and, with W G Grace, the most famous cricketer of them all.

### DR ALAN ROBERTSON

Sir Donald has set a pattern for all who might follow him.

### R C ROBERTSON-GLASGOW

There's nothing new to say about Bradman, anymore than there is about Moiseiwitsch, or the Tower of London.

Bradman was the rarest of Nature's creations, an artist without the handicap of the artistic temperament.

Don Bradman will bat no more against England, and two contrary feelings dispute within us: relief, that our bowlers will no longer be oppressed by the phenomenon; regret, that a miracle has been removed from among us.

Oh, yes; Don's a genius; and geniuses are polygons, with many angles.

When he walked out from the pavilion, rather slowly, with his slight figure and high shoulders, taking it all in under the green big-peaked cap, cricket itself seemed to stand and wait for him.

## WALTER ROBINS

I have known him for many, many years, and no one I can think of has equalled him as a player, as a thinker or as a citizen. He's an astonishing man.

## RAY ROBINSON

*But the vast majority felt that with 'the Don' at the wicket and God in his heaven all was well with the world.*

The chosen of the gods was making others' purple patches look like washed-out lilac.

The living legend will be a fusion of reminiscence, a montage from the mass impressions of those who have watched Bradman, admired his skill, marvelled at him and been puzzled and shocked by him.

## IRVING ROSENWATER

To find the right adjectives to describe his skill and his impact is no more easy today in the quietude of one's home than it was in the hurriedness of the press-boxes of the early 30s.

His dazzling skill literally left some of the critics at a loss for words—and they admitted it.

A Bradman happens once, and it had been heady champagne while it lasted.

Bradman was a miracle in flannels.

. . . all eyes and pens were firmly focused on the Sydney marvel, with the rest of the players satellites revolving around the sun.

All batting was judged in the light of Bradman's mastery: and compared with that, other cricketers were merely human.

Clergymen even preached about Bradman, taking him as their text.

Genius has demonstrated time and again that it is subject to no laws. And the power to surprise—nay, to astound—that Bradman showed in his prime should never be forgotten.

### 'SCONE NEWSPAPER'

And now comes Don Bradman, with all the brilliance of a superb meteor, dazzling the eyes of the world, doing the impossible things . . .

### BRIAN SELLERS

*To say that Don Bradman, even in 1948, was a phenomenon is merely to acknowledge the paucity of one's vocabulary.*

In my opinion, 'the Don' is the greatest player the game as ever seen . . .

### IVAN SHARPE

His feats are marvellous. No other description fits them. Glance over the chief of them.

### SIR GARFIELD SOBERS

A great player will get the bowler to do what he wants him to do by his genius. He will improvise and play unorthodox shots to defeat the field. Don Bradman did that, and he was the greatest of them all.

### REGGIE SPOONER

Don Bradman is a wonderful batsman, a great captain and a most excellent speaker—surely a combination of qualities that is unique.

### 'SPORTING LIFE'

The superb brilliance of Bradman's innings will make it linger long in the memory of those fortunate enough to see it.

### 'SUNDAY TIMES'

In Bradman Australia has a cricket phenomenon—one of the rare miracles of the game—a player who can almost beat a side from his own bat.

### E W SWANTON

But if perfect balance, co-ordination and certainty of execution be accepted as the principal ingredients of batsmanship, we who watched 'the Don' in his early manhood will not hope or expect ever to see its art displayed in a higher form.

### GEOFFREY TEBBUTT

He is not only the outstanding batsman of the day, but the outstanding instance of the cricketer born, as apart from cricketers with a certain amount of natural ability enlarged by tuition, ambition and experience.

More than I have said about Bradman's supreme skill I cannot say. He has been the kind of success beyond the dreams of optimism.

## LORD TENNYSON

His efforts may not be valued by his colossal score; it was the iron discipline of the man, the sacrifice of the real self for his country, his unsuspected patience, the scorn with which he answered his critics that was the wonder, the delight, the masterfulness of his innings; his defiance, his magnetism—that was the mightiness of his conquest.

He is not a run-getting machine; Bradman is a genius.

## GEORGE THATCHER

*One has written so often of Bradman's triumphs that further praise seems superfluous. Bradman is Bradman.*

It is only by comparison that one realises his genius.

## A A THOMSON

*He made runs like a millionaire makes money.*

He was a marvel, a wonder, a nonesuch, and he was his own legend . . .

Rhodes expressed to me an admiration for Bradman that was both sincere and rare in the sense that high praise has always been difficult to extract from him . . . Hobbs, Trumper, and Bradman, and the greatest of these, in his judgement, is Bradman.

. . . an untameable genius was at large, an all-powerful potentate was bending all cricketing nations and all cricketing opponents to his will . . .

. . . for in the heart of 'my' golden age, in W G's late autumn and Hobb's early springtime, there was no single cricketer who stood as high above the rest as did Bradman . . .

But he will gain a respect which will increase and will at last become absolute. That respect Sir Donald Bradman has and will retain.

### 'THE TIMES'

Larwood's fierce attack and the cunning of Verity's spin—and, in the last chapters, Bedser's patient industry—tested his almost inhuman quickness and certainty of reaction, but only to remind spectators that he was a miracle of flesh and blood . . .

To have seen Bradman at the wicket is to have enjoyed the precision of the art of batting.

### BEN TRAVERS

. . . he possesses a brain which would have got him anywhere in any walk of life.

### C T B TURNER

I consider the performances of Don Bradman unique in the history of the game. Whilst it is difficult to make comparisons with other great batsmen, his feats are unparalleled.

### F H TYSON

Bradman was a very hard act to follow. Such was his genius that it appears improbable that the game will ever see his like again.

## UNKNOWN NEWSPAPER

*Such a star rises in the cricket world but once in generations to dim and dominate the deeds of others and leave behind a legacy of astounding achievements.*

## A B E WADDINGTON

Bradman is the greatest batsman I am ever likely to see.

## SIR PELHAM WARNER

I have exhausted my vocabulary of praise in favour of Bradman. There never has been such a batsman.

I am going to suggest that Bradman should present his boots to the English nation. A plaster cast should be made of his feet, for they are the feet of a Genee.

Whatever the cricket historians of the future may say of him, they will surely have to call the period 1928–1948 the 'Bradman Era'.

## C WASHBROOK

As a batsman, Don Bradman was a law unto himself.

I feel sure that Don Bradman's genius as a batsman arose from a remarkably rapid reflex action between his brain and his muscles.

## ROY WEBBER

Lastly, Bradman. What can one say that has not now been said hundreds of times already? Easily the greatest run-scorer that the game has known, he has amassed a great number of records which may never be exceeded.

## TOM WEBSTER

A charming picture of a batsman returning to the pavilion. This is a picture treasured by every member of the English XI. It is Mr Bradman.

## E M WELLINGS

. . . this cricketing genius and great personality, wonderful batsman, superb fielder, and fine captain.

## R S WHITINGTON

And no other batsman flashed quite the kind of lightning with which Bradman illuminated the world.

Millions have shared in the profits of his genius as a cricketer and continue to share in them—as does the game of cricket.

## TREVOR WIGNALL

Pouring praise on Bradman is so much the equivalent of gilding the lily that one hesitates to say much more about him.

Bradman, indeed, has become a menace to the gentlemen of the Press. Even with four dictionaries at our elbows he leaves us gasping.

## 'WISDEN CRICKETERS' ALMANACK'

Still, as a run-getter, he stands alone.

## W M WOODFULL

*He's a freak.*

## F E WOOLLEY

The kind of genius batsman who arrives about once every 20 years or so on purpose to show us which really are the best bowlers.

As in the case of all geniuses, he exercises some kind of hypnotic influence over the bowler.

## R E S WYATT

*He was a genius.*

## 'THE YORKSHIRE POST'

This innings was better than brilliant: it was of such classical accomplishment that it was almost colourless, or rather positively lucid, like a diamond.

There are no adjectives to such a performance, possibly the finest innings ever played . . .

## 'THE OBSERVER'

*When Bradman was gone, the light seemed to go out of the game.*

# INDEX

*229*